BUTCH CASSIDY

BUTCH CASSIDY

Beyond the Grave

W.C. Jameson

TAYLOR TRADE PUBLISHING
Lanham • Boulder • New York • London

Published by Taylor Trade Publishing
An imprint of The Rowman & Littlefield Publishing Group, Inc.
4501 Forbes Boulevard, Suite 200, Lanham, Maryland 20706
www.rowman.com

16 Carlisle Street, London W1D 3BT, United Kingdom

Distributed by NATIONAL BOOK NETWORK

First paperback edition 2012

British Library Cataloguing in Publication Information Available

The hardback edition of this book was previously cataloged by the Library of Congress as follows:

Jameson, W. C., 1942–
Butch Cassidy : beyond the grave / W.C. Jameson.
pages cm
Includes bibliographical references and index.
1. Cassidy, Butch, b. 1866. 2. Outlaws—West (U.S.)—Biography. 3. West (U.S.)—Biography. I. Title.
F595.C362J35 2012
978'.02092—dc23
[B]

2012019750

ISBN 978-1-63076-038-0 (pbk. : alk. paper)
ISBN 978-1-58979-739-0 (cloth : alk. paper)
ISBN 978-1-58979-740-6 (electronic)

Butch Cassidy remained standing next to the Ford coupe, his heart beating fast and heavy with anticipation. For four decades, he had stayed away from his family for fear the presence of an outlaw in their home would bring them shame and they would be ostracized by their neighbors.

After all this time, Cassidy now found himself staring into the face of his beloved father, and the moment filled with certain terror. He wondered if he should just climb back into the car and drive away.

In spite of his fears, Cassidy grinned at the man standing before him. Maxi Parker immediately recognized his firstborn. The two men approached each other and embraced for a long time. With tears in their eyes, they entered the house together.

The outlaw Butch Cassidy had not perished in an alleged South American shootout. He lived to return home to his family.

Contents

Introduction *1*

ONE *Origins* *7*
TWO *Youth* *15*
THREE *Telluride* *21*
FOUR *Enter Butch Cassidy* *29*
FIVE *Prison* *37*
SIX *Robberies* *45*
SEVEN *Enter the Sundance Kid* *57*
EIGHT *Growth of an Outlaw Reputation* *65*
NINE *Betrayal* *71*
TEN *Winnemucca Bank Holdup* *77*
ELEVEN *Eastbound* *81*
TWELVE *South America* *91*
THIRTEEN *The San Vicente Incident* *105*
FOURTEEN *The San Vicente Incident Revisited* *111*
FIFTEEN *Exhumation* *125*
SIXTEEN *Return of the Outlaw, Butch Cassidy* *133*
SEVENTEEN *Enter William T. Phillips* *147*
EIGHTEEN *What Was the Fate of Butch Cassidy?* *155*

Selected Bibliography *175*
Index *181*
About the Author *189*

Introduction

In a variety of ways, the life and times of the outlaw Butch Cassidy remain among the most compelling and mysterious of all of America's Western bad men.

For one thing, Cassidy's outlawry did not result from general meanness or shiftlessness as was often the case with many other notorious crooks of the time. Cassidy's sister, Lula Parker Betenson, once offered the opinion that her brother was not a product of social or personal conflict as were noted outlaws such as Jesse James, the Younger Brothers, the Daltons, and, as some claim, Billy the Kid. Cassidy's lawbreaking activities might have been borne of equal parts mischievousness and youthful boisterousness along with a well-developed disgust and resentment of the manner in which large corporations—banks, railroads, and ranchers—grew wealthy at the expense of the common man and others who possessed little in the way of power, prestige, or money. Cassidy's disgust might have led to a desire for revenge, or perhaps at the very least a perceived need to remind the moneyed interests from time to time that they could be thwarted.

A certain level of idealism likely pervaded Cassidy's thoughts and actions. To many, he was perceived as the Robin Hood of his time—taking from the rich and distributing the booty among those who needed it. Such romantic images are often attached to outlaws but are seldom true. In Cassidy's case, however, there might indeed be some element of truth to this notion, although it is well known that this interesting bandit enjoyed spending money on himself as well.

One Cassidy researcher, Lula Parker Betenson, wrote that Butch may have perceived himself as a small-time cattleman or horseman and regarded the large cattle corporations, banks, and railroads as threats to his way of life. Betenson stated that Cassidy was "a product of the great land, the big sky, the wide open spaces" and that he just as easily could have been a congressman or senator.

Betenson's romantic inclinations aside, it is possible that Cassidy simply delighted in robbing banks, trains, and payrolls, not only because he achieved some sense of revenge, but also because he enjoyed and profited from the fruits of such activity. As Butch Cassidy grew proficient at his chosen occupation, there is little doubt that he continued to rob because he needed or wanted money. Cassidy's outlaw activities were generally associated with cattle rustling, horse theft, bank robberies, train robberies, and payroll robberies. In virtually every case, however, his targets were large corporations. While he made a living taking money from them, most believe he derived greatest satisfaction from creating difficulties for these economic entities.

The fact remains, Cassidy could have accomplished such goals in far less risky ways than taking on members of the American Bankers Association, the Union Pacific Railroad, and large cattle empires in Wyoming, Utah, and Colorado.

It appears as if Cassidy was simply determined to create as much misery and as many problems for the big corporations as possible. That his activities were against the law did not seem to faze him, as his respect for the law had been deeply wounded.

There is also abundant evidence that Butch Cassidy's disappointment and disgust for power and authority was also directed at the Mormon church because of the injustices it inflicted on his family.

With regard to Cassidy's Robin Hood image, there exists indisputable evidence that he often went out of his way to help those less fortunate than he, and the tales of him delivering medicines to the sick and providing help for the elderly and infirm are legion.

Unlike many outlaws, the evidence is clear that Cassidy, though successful at his chosen field of outlawry, never visited physical harm on a single soul. During the commission of his bank and train robberies, the customers and passengers were never molested and their valuables never taken from them, at least not by Cassidy himself. In one case, Cassidy is known to have admonished a gang member for harming an innocent bystander. Hurting someone, stated one of his acquaintances, was simply not a part of his character.

Cassidy, the person and the outlaw, remains enigmatic. While there is no denying that he perpetrated a number of major bank and train robberies, as well as other depredations, it is likely he has been given far more credit for such activities than he deserved. Research shows this is true with most famous outlaws.

After Cassidy's name became a household word in Colorado, Wyoming, and Utah during the 1890s, nearly every misdeed committed in the region was subsequently attributed to him, even when it was proven he was far away from the crime scene at the time. The same is true relative to his stay in South America. Many of the Western-style robberies that took place in Argentina, Bolivia, and Chile between 1904 and 1908 were attributed to Cassidy and his companions. Where there is ample evidence that he did commit several holdups, many, if not most, of those reported were the work of others emulating techniques employed by Cassidy and the Wild Bunch. Though guilty of breaking the law on numerous occasions, a number of the deeds attributed to Butch Cassidy carry with them no solid evidence whatsoever that he was actually involved.

As an outlaw, Cassidy's mannerisms and demeanor were unlike those of other noted outlaws. He has never been described as vicious, vengeful, mean, a killer, or even a particularly bad man. On the contrary, when acquaintances and contemporaries of Cassidy were asked to describe him, mostly they offered adjectives such as intelligent, generous, pleasant, outgoing, friendly, happy-go-lucky, charming, boyish, well mannered, and polite, as well as having a fine sense of humor.

As mysterious and elusive as his life was, the death of Butch Cassidy is considerably more so. The popular and traditionally accepted belief is that Cassidy, in the company of Harry Longabaugh, the Sundance Kid, was killed in a shootout with soldiers in the small Bolivian town of San Vicente in 1908, a few days following the robbery of a mine payroll. The original inspiration for this version of the demise of Cassidy was published in a magazine some twenty-two years *after* the event by a writer who got his information secondhand from a man who was not present at the event and who was subsequently suspected of making such a claim in order to protect Cassidy, who was his friend.

This perception that Cassidy and the Sundance Kid were killed in a Bolivian shootout has been perpetuated over the years, in large part as a result of the 1969 William Goldman film, *Butch Cassidy and the Sundance Kid*, starring the charismatic Paul Newman as Cassidy and Robert Redford as the Sundance Kid. A significant number of researchers and investigators who have studied the events surrounding Cassidy's alleged demise in South America have concluded that it simply did not happen.

There are some who still cling to the unsubstantiated notion that Cassidy, along with the Sundance Kid, died in Bolivia in 1908. Regardless, there is neither conclusive nor substantive evidence that it happened. In addition, and correlatively, there remains no conclusive evidence that Butch Cassidy and the Sundance Kid participated in the payroll robbery attributed to them; there is no clear documentation that it was Cassidy and Longabaugh who arrived in the small Bolivian town of San Vicente where they were allegedly gunned down; there is no solid evidence that Cassidy and his friend were killed in San Vicente at all or, for that matter, in South America; there exists no significant evidence that the two bandits were buried in the local cemetery, as claimed by some.

Efforts to determine the validity of any of the aforementioned claims have never resulted in the accumulation of any logical or compelling evidence for such, much less proof.

On the other hand, there exists some compelling and hard-to-dismiss evidence that the outlaw Butch Cassidy survived his South American adventures and returned to the United States to visit family and friends and, according to at least one researcher, settled down with a wife and adopted child in Spokane, Washington.

Many maintain that the evidence for Cassidy's return to the United States after his alleged death is far more convincing than the somewhat questionable evidence associated with his demise in South America. As much as is practical, prevailing arguments for both will be presented in the following pages so that the reader may be in a position of making a determination one way or the other, or neither.

As with many efforts associated with the search for truth as it relates to outlaws of the American West, the researcher is often confronted with confusing, conflicting, contradictory, partially valid, and sometimes fanciful accounts. Myths and folklore regarding outlaw figures are far too often accepted as truths, much of which gets published and generally accepted by the public. For example, the popular image of the outlaw Billy the Kid is known to most through dime novelists and the largely erroneous biography penned by Sheriff Pat Garrett and his friend, Ashmon Upson.

Other obstacles confronting the serious researcher include overt resistance from hobbyists, enthusiasts, and history buffs, as well as a few credentialed historians, to any change in the popular version of Cassidy's death. For the most part, many of them appear to be quite rigid in their adherence to the popular mythology and have manifested reluctance to even consider evidence to the contrary.

One of the earliest books about Butch Cassidy and the Wild Bunch was penned by Charles Kelly in 1938. Much of what was contained in Kelly's book, *The Outlaw Trail: A History of Butch Cassidy and His Wild Bunch*, has since been found to be in error or highly questionable. As a Butch Cassidy researcher, Kelly has long been discredited. In his favor, Kelly accumulated a great deal of Cassidy information and conducted a number of important interviews. Unfortunately, Kelly did little to separate fact from fiction—it was clear that he, like many enthusiasts, simply lacked the necessary investigative and analytical skills to do so. Unfortunately, subsequent writers and filmmakers relied heavily on Kelly's work. In spite of the truths that have been revealed since its publication, many still rely on *The Outlaw Trail.*

In recent times, some of the most impressively researched works on Butch Cassidy have been conducted by Ann Meadows (*Digging Up Butch and Sundance*, 1996) and Larry Pointer (*In Search of Butch Cassidy*, 1977). *Butch Cassidy: A Biography* by Richard Patterson (1998), though often criticized, is a solid, comprehensive work that includes many facets of this interesting and noted outlaw.

In the following pages, the reader will be introduced to the traditional Butch Cassidy, the theoretical Butch Cassidy, and the man who "became" Butch Cassidy after 1908. Cassidy's origins and youth, as well as information relative to his ventures into outlawry and related motives, will be presented. As much as is possible when treating data and information that is, in some cases, well over a century old, this book provides nuances of the Cassidy personality as it has been attested to by family and friends, a personality that might figure heavily into explaining things such as his penchant for robbing banks and trains, as well to several aspects of his alleged return.

Thanks to the efforts of a number of competent researchers, a great deal of information relating to Cassidy's life and times in South America is presented herein, particularly his life leading up to the so-called San Vicente shootout.

The evidence for and against Cassidy's survival of the South American episode and his alleged return to the United States is examined.

Finally, this book evaluates the man many Cassidy researchers believe was the famous outlaw who returned to the American West.

Did Butch Cassidy, noted outlaw of the American West, survive his alleged death at the hands of Bolivian soldiers in 1908 and return to friends and family in the United States? The evidence that suggests he did is impressive and not easily dismissed, but how he lived and which identity he assumed are still being debated.

Read for yourself and decide.

ONE

Origins

The noted American outlaw who came to be known as Butch Cassidy was born Robert LeRoy Parker on April 13, 1866, in Beaver, Utah. His origins and boyhood were atypical of most bad men: he was born into a loving and devoted Mormon family and raised to be loyal and honest. While family influences always remained strong, the attraction of the church diminished in a dramatic fashion.

Cassidy's parents, Maximillian and Ann Parker, were Mormons, as were their parents. Maximillian was the son of Robert and Ann Hartley Parker, English immigrants who encountered a variety of hardships and trials as well as successes in their new Utah homeland.

Robert and Ann Hartley Parker were both born in Burnley, Lancashire County, England. Robert was well educated according to the standards of the day. He took up weaving as a trade and in a short time became quite accomplished. He met his future wife, Ann, in a textile mill.

In 1836, Robert Parker was first exposed to the tenets and rituals of the Mormon church. The organization's missionaries to England had been conducting seminars on the relatively new denomination. Robert regularly attended the meetings, quickly became convinced it was the one true church, and joined. Ann was not as enthusiastic as Parker about the "Saints," as the members called themselves, but, employing their philosophy, he worked hard to convince her it was the only way to get to heaven. Because she loved him she listened to his ideas about the new church. She grew proud of Robert's passion and commitment. With his encouragement, Ann converted to the Mormon faith despite the wishes of her parents. Shortly after her baptism in 1843, she and Robert were married.

One year later, Robert and Ann gave birth to a son they named Maximillian. During the next eleven years, five more children were born to the Parkers, and the family eventually moved to the town of Preston in Lancashire County, located just a few miles west of Burnley.

Across the Atlantic Ocean in America, the Mormon church was experiencing serious difficulties. As a result of numerous conflicts with the dominant Christian denominations, some of them physical and violent, the Saints had been driven from their settlements and forced to find homes elsewhere. As they moved westward, they were likewise challenged. It was often made known they were not wanted. In some cases, they were attacked and their homes burned. Some of the Saints were even killed.

Eventually, under the leadership of the self-anointed prophet Brigham Young, the Saints journeyed to and settled in the valley of the Great Salt Lake in what would eventually become the state of Utah. Following the initial phase of settlement, Young sent word to the church's missionaries in England, Denmark, and Sweden to encourage tradesmen to come to America and assist in the building of what he perceived would be the new Mormon empire.

Robert Parker contemplated the invitation to go to America, weighing the advantages and disadvantages. He knew if he heeded the call to the mission, he would sorely miss England, his relatives, and friends, but his commitment to the church was strong and growing.

Meanwhile, Robert's job at the textile mill in the nearby town of Preston provided ample support for his family. For a time, young Maximillian, still a mere boy, was put to work in the mill. Unlike his father, Maxi, as he was called, hated the work. The drudgery and tedium of the repetitious tasks was not at all to his liking. One day, to the embarrassment of his father, Maxi simply walked away from the job. Though punished severely by the elder Parker, young Maxi refused to return to the mill.

By this time, Robert Parker was an elder in the Mormon church and the head of a small mission in Preston. After lengthy deliberation and prayer, he ultimately decided the best thing for him and his growing family was to heed the call from Brigham Young and go to America. His skills as a weaver would be invaluable, and he was convinced the move would provide opportunities for his children they would not have in England.

Robert sold his home, his furniture, and his small herd of cattle to raise the price of boat fare to America. On March 22, 1856, the entire Parker family boarded a ship, the *Enoch Train*, for the United States. With the Parkers were approximately 530 other Mormon immigrants, all ultimately bound for the region of the Great Salt Lake in Utah. The passage took five weeks. The ship finally arrived in Boston on April 30. Maxi was twelve years of age when he first stepped onto the shores of his new country. Following a trip to New York City, the group of Mormons boarded a train for Iowa City, Iowa, arriving May 12.

At Iowa City, the immigrants became part of a group historians have since labeled the Handcart Pioneers. Here, they spent approximately one month in preparation for the long trip across the plains and mountains. Generally, wagon trains had been the normal mode of transporting groups of people to California and points in between. For reasons not entirely clear, leader Brigham Young was convinced simple handcarts would be faster and easier than wagons. These large, two-wheeled wagons were fitted with a pair of long poles that extended forward. A Saint would position himself or herself between the poles, strap on a harness similar to one designed for a mule, lift, and pull. Young reasoned that few of the Saints had enough money to purchase teams of oxen or mules. He also assumed and claimed they knew little about how to handle such animals. Furthermore, Young did not want the members of his flock spending their savings on what he considered expensive wagons and stock. He told them they needed to carry their savings with them to their destination.

A large number of the handcarts were hastily constructed with green, unseasoned wood and poorly fashioned for such a long and rugged journey. As the lumber dried out in the arid environments of the West, many wagons broke apart, forcing migrants to abandon precious belongings along the trail and take only what they could carry on their backs.

The first group of Handcart Pioneers, some 274 strong, departed Iowa City on June 9. The second group, called the MacArthur Company, left two days later and included 221 Mormons, among them the Parker family. While Robert pulled and young Maxi pushed the cart, the rest of the family walked alongside. In that manner they covered hundreds of miles across unfamiliar terrain.

Late on the afternoon of July 1, the Parker family experienced disaster. As the adults of the MacArthur Company set up camp for the night and prepared dinner, the children scattered throughout the adjacent countryside to play. A sudden thundershower, however, sent them hurrying back to camp. As the Parker children gathered near the family cart in the pouring rain, Ann Parker noticed that Arthur, the fourth child, was missing. None of the other children remembered seeing him and a search was undertaken, one that extended well into the night and most of the following day. In spite of the missing child, the leader of the company, Elder MacArthur, ordered the party to pack up and continue their journey.

After packing his wagon, Robert Parker sent his family along with the others and remained alone to continue the search for his son. Just before parting, Ann handed her husband a red shawl, telling him that if he found the child he was to wave it so she would know he was all right.

For two more days, the Handcart Pioneers trudged westward. Ann Parker constantly scanned the trail behind them searching for sign of her husband and son. At night she prayed and cried, fearing the two had been captured or killed by Indians.

On the evening of July 5 after camp was made and dinner served, Ann Parker walked to a low knoll where she knelt and prayed. When she had finished and rose to return to camp, she detected something moving in the distance far to the east. Though it was dusk and the light was dim, she recognized her husband's gait. As she squinted into the distance, she saw another figure, this one smaller and wrapped in a red shawl, walking alongside Robert. It was Arthur. Her prayers had been answered.

On July 15, another handcart company departed Iowa City for the valley of the Great Salt Lake. In this company was the Gillies family, originally from Scotland but most recently from England—Robert and Jane and their four children Moroni, Daniel, Christina, and Annie. Like the Parkers, the Gillies family converted to the Mormon faith while residing in England. As with the MacArthur Company that departed over a month earlier, this one faced similar tedium and the dangers of the long journey, including drought, Indians, and the deterioration of the poorly constructed handcarts. The company in which the Gillies traveled also ran low on food, and eventually each member was rationed less than one-half pound of flour per day.

The MacArthur party of English, Danish, and Swedish converts crossed the Missouri River during late August 1856. Men, women, and children alike had long since tired of walking and pulling their belongings in the handcarts. They were also tiring of the fare; biscuits or corn bread and salt pork comprised almost every meal. As the hopes of the travelers flagged, Elder MacArthur tried to keep their spirits up, telling them the promised land of the valley of the Great Salt Lake was not far away.

The party with which the Parkers traveled was still a long way from their goal when it was struck by October snowstorms along the eastern slopes of the Rocky Mountains. By the time they reached South Pass in Wyoming, blizzard-like conditions accompanied by temperatures well below zero and deep, nearly impassable snow drifts severely hampered travel and were responsible for a number of deaths. Of the approximately three thousand members of the church who undertook the 1,300-mile journey from Iowa City to the valley of the Great Salt Lake, at least 250 perished along the way.

Robert and Ann Parker, along with their children, survived the terrible weather and continued their journey, walking and pulling their cart to Utah along with the surviving Mormon faithful. Eager to help, young Maximillian, still only twelve years old, did more than his share. On September 26, 1856, following over one hundred days of toil, they finally arrived at the valley of the Great Salt Lake. Seven members of the MacArthur Company died along the trail.

An oft-told tale relative to the Parker journey overland to Salt Lake City has the elder Parker dying. In *The Outlaw Trail: A History of Butch Cassidy and His Wild Bunch*, originally published in 1938, Charles Kelly wrote, "Being one of the strongest men in the party, he was given a position well in the lead, where he helped break trail through deep snowdrifts." Kelly goes on to relate that the "strenuous exertions on behalf of his starving and freezing family finally sapped his strength, and one bitter cold morning he was found dead in his blankets, almost within sight of the warm valley of the Green River."

Kelly's yarn is characteristic of what many people think they know about Butch Cassidy's origins. This tale, while certainly a dramatic and somewhat romantic one, lacks anything to do with the truth. Poorly researched publications such as Kelly's have continued to generate misunderstanding relative to the lives and times of American outlaws in general and Butch Cassidy in particular.

A few weeks after completing their journey to Salt Lake City, the Parkers moved to a new settlement called American Fork, located approximately twenty-five miles to the south. Here, Robert Parker taught school for a time. Since there was a need for weavers, the church eventually encouraged him to move to the town of Beaver, some 175 miles south-southwest of Salt Lake City, where he went to work in a woolen mill, putting his weaving skills to good use. For a time, according to some researchers, young Maxi worked in the mill but, as in England, despised the tedium. As before, he ran away.

Since winter was well under way in southern Utah and the Parkers had no time to construct a suitable cabin, they moved into a dugout. Life for the family that winter was miserable as the thatched, dirt roof leaked and rainwater and snowmelt poured into the pitiful dwelling. Many times, water collected on the floor and turned it into mud.

Some time later, the Gillies family, having successfully completed the long journey to Salt Lake City, was also assigned to Beaver. The church determined that Robert Gillies's skills as a carpenter and cabinetmaker were sorely needed in that region.

When he grew older, young Maximillian was later appointed by the Mormon church to help guide additional wagon trains from St. Louis, Missouri, to the valley of the Great Salt Lake. He also worked for a time as a mailman. It has also been written that he served for a time in what has since come to be called the Black Hawk War, a series of skirmishes between Mormons and a loose confederation of Utes, Paiutes, and some Navajos led by Chief Black Hawk.

Being residents of the same small town, it was inevitable that Maxi Parker would meet Annie Gillies. Though her real name was Annie, Maxi called her Ann. Ann was described as "a pretty, charming lass," and she and young Maxi soon became friends and playmates.

In 1865, when Robert and Ann Parker were sent by the church to help operate a new cotton mill constructed in Washington, Utah, Maxi stayed behind. According to his daughter Lula Parker Betenson, Maxi "had eyes only for Annie and wasn't about to take chances on losing her." The two were married on July 12, 1865. The first of thirteen children, Robert LeRoy Parker, destined to become the most famous member of the family, was born on April 13, 1866, according to Parker family documents.

Robert and Ann Parker traveled the eighty miles from their home in Washington, Utah, to be present at the birth of their grandchild. Also present were the maternal grandparents, Robert and Jane Sinclair Gillies. The elder Parker held the baby Robert in his arms as the newborn was blessed and given his name.

During his tenure as a mailman, Maxi often crossed Circle Valley, a broad, flat plain surrounded by mountains and through which ran the Sevier River. He was convinced the fertile land was quite suitable for growing crops and raising cattle. Importantly for Maxi, it looked like a fine place to raise a family.

Maxi eventually purchased 160 acres in the valley from a man named James. The property was located some three miles south of Circleville, a small settlement near the confluence of Cottonwood Creek and the Sevier River, consisting of little more than a few Mormon residences and a schoolhouse. As soon as he was able, Parker moved his wife and six children into a two-room log cabin constructed near the base of a hill. The year was 1879, and young Robert was thirteen years old.

One room of the cabin served as kitchen and living area, and the entire Parker family slept in the other, their beds being little more than pallets made from ticking stuffed with straw and corn husks. The floor was also covered with straw that, in turn, was topped with cloths and homemade rag carpets. Over time, a separate kitchen and two bedrooms were added.

During the first year on the property, Maxi cleared the land, dug canals, and planted crops. His first agricultural effort yielded wheat, and despite high winds and other weather problems, he managed a harvest.

The family endured freezing winters, severe droughts, and occasional floods. During the harsh winter of 1879–1880, they lost all but two of their cows, a disaster from which it took years to recover. But recover they did, and during the process Maxi managed to homestead additional property, adding more land to the family's holdings.

To help make ends meet, Maxi went to work cutting mine timbers at Frisco, a small mining town located just west of Beaver. He also hauled wood for charcoal near St. George, about one hundred miles from Circle Valley. In time, the Parker family grew to fourteen children.

During this period, squatters were becoming a growing problem in that part of Utah. It was only a matter of time until Parker was forced to deal with them. Another family of Mormons had settled onto a portion of the new Parker homestead and began tilling the land and grazing livestock. Because little in the way of formal law enforcement existed in the region, and because Maxi was committed to following the rules established by the Mormon church, he reported the trespass to the local bishop and requested the squatters be required to leave. In a surprising decision, the bishop judged the newcomers more deserving of the land than Parker and awarded it to them.

Parker had spent years, along with a great deal of energy and money, building this portion of his ranch only to have it taken away from him by the church authorities. Though Ann Parker was a devoted member of the faith, Maxi was lax about attending services. He also smoked cigarettes, which violated the rules of the Mormon church. Parker was convinced taking his land away from him was the church's way of punishing him for his perceived transgressions. Angered by the unfair judgment, Maximillian Parker had little to do with the Mormon church thereafter.

In spite of the setback, Parker remained a hardworking rancher and a good husband and father. As soon as he was old enough, young Robert began accompanying his father and helping with the chores.

Robert Parker reveled in the time he spent with his father and in many ways patterned himself after Maxi. From his father, young Parker learned much about loyalty, a trait that characterized him in later years. He also learned about the value and virtue of hard work and completing a task. In time, he also came to share many more of his father's attitudes, particularly those relating to the Mormon church.

Robert also adored his mother and his siblings. He constantly saw to their welfare, entertained them, took them for horseback rides, found pets for them, and generally worked to be a contributing member of the large family.

According to one researcher, young Robert Parker remained loyal to the Mormon church, even continuing to tithe the required 10 percent throughout his life. Most, however, do not share this contention. According to Robert's sister, Lula Parker Betenson, the young boy stopped attending church services and, like his father, harbored contempt for the Mormon church as well as a disdain for religious hypocrites in general for the rest of his life.

Robert LeRoy Parker, a smiling and happy son of Utah, was a third-generation Mormon and a member of a somewhat prominent family. This same lad who loved his family so much and was the pride of relatives and peers would grow up to become Butch Cassidy, noted rustler, train robber, and bank robber and one of America's most famous outlaws.

TWO

Youth

Little is known about or even particularly noteworthy of Robert LeRoy Parker's early youth save for his strong attachment to his family, a singular difficulty with the law, and a chance encounter with a man who was to influence him for the rest of his life.

As young Robert grew up in the close-knit and hardworking Parker family, he reveled in the association with his father and enjoyed working side by side with him on the ranch. At an early age, Robert developed a fascination with horses that eventually led to the development of remarkable skills as they related to breaking, training, and riding. Even as an early teenager, young Parker manifested this talent.

As the oldest child, Robert LeRoy Parker had a well-developed sense of responsibility and a special fondness and affection for his siblings. He often played with his brothers and sisters, and sometimes entertained them by performing tunes on the harmonica. In addition to his own family, other area youngsters enjoyed young Parker and often sought him out. With his own family, as well as with children of neighboring ranchers, Parker was easygoing and patient.

As he grew into his teenage years, the towheaded youth exhibited the deep-set blue eyes and square jaw of his mother. From his father, he inherited a sense of humor, determination, and dependability.

Robert LeRoy Parker was a mere thirteen years of age when he experienced his first encounter with the law. Unfortunately for him, it turned out to be a negative one. At the time, he was working for a rancher named Pat Ryan not far from the town of Milford, located approximately forty miles northwest of Circleville. The Parker family had debts to pay, and in addition to farming and ranching, Maxi had taken on additional work cutting railroad ties and hauling timber. To help with the family expenses, young Robert decided to contribute, and he eventually secured a job on the Ryan Ranch. Ryan quickly grew impressed with the boy. Robert proved early he was capable of doing a man's work, and he was dependable and intelligent.

One payday, Robert decided he needed a new pair of overalls, so he rode into Milford to make the purchase. On arriving at the mercantile store, he was mildly annoyed to find it closed. Having already made the long journey into town and, not wanting to wait around for the owner to return, Parker gained entrance, selected a pair of overalls, and left a note promising to return another day with payment for the pants.

This act, conducted with all the best intentions, was unacceptable to the store owner who immediately reported it as a theft. Two days later, lawmen arrested Parker. After the details were sorted out and it was eventually determined no serious crime had been committed, the youth was released.

The incident left several important impressions on the boy. For the most part, he was concerned that the allegation of theft was embarrassing for his family, and he regretted the shame it may have cast upon them. Additionally, even though he was young and inexperienced in such things, Parker remained appalled at what he considered a bullying miscarriage of justice and appeared from that point on to harbor certain contempt for the law. Because he was brought up by his family to be honest and forthcoming, he presumed in his youthful naïveté that everyone else was also, that others would understand and appreciate such things in their fellow man. The boy's lack of worldly experience was in part responsible for his cultivation of this embryonic idealism. This was soon to change.

Author Charles Kelly provides a somewhat different explanation of Parker's first brush with the law. Based on an alleged interview with a former Juab County sheriff, Kelly determined Parker had been arrested for stealing a saddle. While in jail, the boy was "mistreated by the sheriff of Garfield County." Angered by his treatment, Parker, according to Kelly, swore vengeance then and forevermore against lawmen. There is no evidence that such a thing actually happened.

Following his employment at the Ryan Ranch, Robert, along with his mother and two brothers, soon found work closer to home at the Marshall Ranch and Dairy around 1881 or 1882. Initially, Maxi was not in favor of the arrangement but was finally persuaded when he became convinced that the extra money earned, along with free milk, cheese, and butter, would help get them back on their feet. Kelly wrote that Maxi Parker actually purchased the Marshall Ranch, but the majority of Cassidy scholars are in agreement that neither evidence nor likelihood of such a thing happening was apparent.

According to local gossip recorded by some researchers, the Marshall Ranch occasionally served as headquarters for gangs of horse thieves and cattle rustlers. One of the outlaws who frequented the ranch was a man named Mike Cassidy, who, some say, was the generally acknowledged leader of the rustlers. It was at the Marshall Ranch during his second year of employment that Robert Parker met Mike Cassidy. The event amounted to a significant turning point in the life of the boy.

Mike Cassidy was many things. He was a competent cowhand with years of experience with horses. Cassidy was well known throughout the region for his skills in breaking horses and often found himself in demand with area ranchers. Cassidy was also highly skilled with a pistol. He was considered a marksman who allegedly could place a bullet through a silver dollar at forty paces.

Mike Cassidy was charismatic. A likeable man, he was often idolized by area youth who considered him a kind of hero. He was well liked and respected by the group of cowboys he associated with and never lacked for friends.

Mike Cassidy was also an outlaw. He was known to be a cattle rustler and a horse thief. It is maintained by some historians that while working at the Marshall place Cassidy continued stealing horses and cattle from other ranchers. In fact, he held a large herd of his own in Bryce Canyon, a rugged, dissected maze of sandstone canyons located some sixty miles to the southeast.

Some have argued about the legitimacy of Mike Cassidy's reputation as an outlaw: A few have claimed he was, pure and simple, one who broke the law. Others attribute to him a certain prankishness modified by a skewed perception of what justice actually was, or should have been. In truth, the West was filling up with railroaders and cattle barons, leaving very little land for men and families of modest means. The smaller ranchers and cattlemen, such as Cassidy, often roped and branded strays, called mavericks, from the larger herds owned by the corporate ranchers. In many parts of the country, such activity was recognized and accepted, and the mavericker assumed a few cattle here and there would not be missed. Men like Mike Cassidy regarded the strays as the price the larger cattle ranchers had to pay for pushing the smaller operators out.

However, the wealthy cattlemen held the money and the power. They were capable of manipulating laws and lawmen to serve their own interests, and often did. For many, mavericking was not tolerated. Soon the mavericks were deemed nothing more than common rustlers who were hunted down and sometimes hung on the spot.

It has never been entirely clear whether or not Mike Cassidy was simply a hardworking cattleman trying his best to get ahead or if he was little more than a common cattle thief. In any case, he often found himself at odds with laws and lawmen.

Like other young men, Robert LeRoy Parker was attracted to Mike Cassidy from the very first time he met him at the Marshall Ranch. Parker was impressed with the older cowboy's skills with livestock. It may be assumed that he also admired the experienced cowman's attitude relative to the wealthy cattle barons.

The outlaw's life must have seemed quite glamorous to the young Parker. It was a life filled with excitement and a certain level of danger, whereas Parker's was one filled with menial duties, hard work, and growing boredom. Author Larry Pointer wrote that it was no small stretch for Parker "to rationalize Cassidy's rustling as retribution for the transgressions of religious hypocrites and greedy land barons."

The outlaw Mike Cassidy likewise took a liking to Parker. He was impressed with the youth's already well-developed skills with livestock. During the days of their relationship on the Marshall Ranch, Cassidy passed along much of his knowledge and technique of horse breaking and training to the boy. Cassidy gave Parker a saddle and spent time teaching him the fine points of horsemanship. In a short time, Robert LeRoy Parker was almost as good a horseman as Cassidy.

Cassidy also gave Parker a pistol, along with money for cartridges. When time was available, he taught the youngster how to handle the weapon. Before long, Parker was nearly the marksman Cassidy was known to be. By the time he was sixteen years of age, the youngster could shoot with remarkable accuracy, even from the back of a galloping horse. With the passage of several weeks, Parker was regarded as the best shot in the valley, replacing Mike Cassidy with that distinction.

When Cassidy's herd of stolen cattle became too large to be contained by the Bryce Canyon environs, he decided to move them to the Henry Mountains, another sixty miles to the southeast, near the Colorado River. In need of some extra cowhands to work the herd, it is believed that he asked young Parker to go along. The experience, if it actually happened, likely further solidified the relationship between the two, and Parker probably learned even more about handling livestock and shooting a gun.

A short time later, Mike Cassidy ran afoul of the law again. He fled to Mexico where, according to most reports, he remained until he died.

The growing relationship between the boy Robert LeRoy Parker and the outlaw Mike Cassidy did not go unnoticed by Ann Parker. Concerned that the two were spending far too much time together, and worried about the potentially harmful influence the outlaw could have on her son, she eventually moved Robert and his two brothers back to Circleville.

In spite of his mother's concerns and admonitions, young Parker maintained contact with Mike Cassidy for a time. Several months later, when Cassidy indicated he would be leaving the Marshall Ranch and moving on, Parker asked to accompany him. Perhaps aware of the concern evinced by the boy's mother, and perhaps in a sincere attempt to keep the youth from going astray, Cassidy discouraged him. He counseled Parker to remain with his family.

With the continuous hard work on ranches, and with constantly practicing his horsemanship skills, Parker's frame filled out with hard muscle. When he was eighteen years of age, he was five feet nine inches tall and weighed approximately 155 pounds. Though strong and durable, Parker remained soft spoken and friendly to all. He was characterized as having a disarmingly charming smile and was quick to laugh and generally liked. He continued to be regarded as dependable, hardworking, and loyal to his employers and to his friends.

Though Mike Cassidy had departed, Parker was still guided by many of the lessons he learned from the older cowboy. Though he was unable to follow Cassidy at the time, he did so later, at least figuratively.

Shortly after turning eighteen years of age in 1884, Robert told his mother he was leaving, that he needed to find opportunities above and beyond those offered at the southern Utah ranch. He spoke of traveling to Telluride, Colorado, and finding a job in the mines.

According to his sister, Lula Parker Betenson, on the day Robert decided to leave, his father was working at some distant location. His mother carefully packed him a supply of provisions and rolled them into a blue woolen blanket his grandfather had made for him when Robert was a baby.

As Robert saddled his horse, the family dog, Dash, grew excited at the prospect of going along, as was his custom on the ranch. Robert asked his mother to hold the dog so he wouldn't follow. After mounting his mare, Babe, and taking the reins of his colt, Cornish, Robert LeRoy Parker rode away from the family homestead.

According to writer Richard Patterson, Mormons had a tradition of planting Lombardy poplar trees wherever they settled. Years earlier, Robert and his mother worked together to plant a row of poplars along the path that led to the main road. As he now rode down the path, Robert remembered that time of planting as he passed the line of trees.

The incident was to be recalled forty years later.

THREE

Telluride

Robert LeRoy Parker had been gone from Circle Valley for several months when Maxi rode into the town of Circleville one day to purchase some supplies. While there, he received some troubling news. Maxi learned that several of the area cattle ranchers had discovered some of their stock had turned up in a herd belonging to two companions of Mike Cassidy. The two men, however, produced bills of sale for the cattle. According to the documents, the seller was none other than Robert LeRoy Parker.

Maxi met with area constable James Wiley, who offered some explanation. Robert, knowing he was going to be leaving the area, apparently agreed to put his name on the phony bills of sale. The two friends who had possession of the herd had families to support and wished to remain living in the region, and Robert may have simply wanted to help them. As it eventually turned out, the stolen cattle were returned to their rightful owners, the two friends of Cassidy were not suspected of doing anything illegal, and Robert Parker had fled the jurisdiction of the state. There was little the constable could, or wanted to, do.

In signing the phony bills of sale, Robert may not have overtly intended anything illegal. Perhaps the rather naïve youth was completely unaware of the ultimate consequences of his act. It is doubtful that criminal mischief was his motivation, but at the very least his action indicated a serious lack of judgment. Because of the incident, however, Robert was now known in the community as a criminal. A seed for his eventual reputation as an outlaw had been planted.

When Robert LeRoy Parker rode into Telluride, Colorado, in the summer of 1884, he was eighteen. Once known as Columbia, the town was reveling in a successful gold mining boom. Tons of ore were being dug from the mountainsides, and poor men became wealthy almost overnight. The name Telluride came from tellurium, a semimetallic element related to selenium and sulphur and considered one of the most important elements found in combination with gold. Telluride was located at the bottom of a deep canyon in a location known as San Miguel Park.

During its peak, the town of Telluride was referred to by many as the Sodom of the American West. Telluride offered numerous diversions for the hardworking miners—saloons, dance halls, whorehouses, and gambling dens abounded. Killings and robberies were a common occurrence, many of them going unsolved. Mercantiles and supply stores were everywhere, and large amounts of money changed hands around the clock.

In a short time, Robert, who by this time was calling himself Roy, secured a job some distance from Telluride. He was hired to pack ore onto mules and escort them from the mines to the mills. The days were long and hard, but Roy, always a hard worker, reveled in it at first. He also made good money for the first time in his life. A portion of his paycheck was sent home, but the saloons and women of Telluride accounted for much of the rest.

Not long after his arrival in Telluride, Roy sold his mare and made an arrangement with a local rancher to keep his unbroken colt, Cornish. The demands of his job prevented Roy from spending much time with the colt, and his visits to the animal were rare.

During the first spring following his arrival, Roy decided it was time to break the colt, so he visited more and more. With each visit, the rancher made an offer to purchase the animal, but Roy always turned him down.

One evening after work, Roy went down to the pasture, removed the three-year-old colt, and took him elsewhere to break. The rancher charged Roy Parker with horse theft and asked the town police chief to place him under arrest. The rancher stated that the colt belonged to him and could provide several witnesses to support his claim.

Roy decided it was time to leave. He rode away to the northwest and was arrested a short time later and placed in the county jail at Montrose, located about forty miles north of Telluride. A few of Roy's friends, convinced he was innocent, sent a wire to Maxi explaining the situation. Maxi left immediately for Montrose to try to help his son.

During the subsequent trial, Roy was found not guilty. Following his courtroom experience, Robert was urged by his father to return with him to Circleville. Roy refused, explaining that he felt trapped in Utah, that he had few opportunities beyond the dullness of working on a ranch. He longed for adventure and excitement, and it was not to be found in the Mormon communities of Utah. Maxi returned alone.

A short time after Roy was found innocent of stealing his own horse, he departed Telluride and traveled to Wyoming, earning his living by taking odd jobs. Not only was he eager to leave the town in which he was nearly judged a criminal, but also he was still searching for adventure. In the spring of 1887, he wound up in Miles City, Montana. Life in Wyoming and Montana was not what he expected. He suffered one employment disappointment after another. After a time, he realized he missed the excitement of Telluride and the prospects of making money. He made the decision to return to Colorado.

The year was 1888. Soon after arriving in Telluride a second time, Roy found employment. Unfortunately, he returned to another job with long hours. Though he was making money, he quickly grew bored with the day-to-day drudgery of earning a living. He had not been back in town long when he met Matt Warner, an adventurous, free-living person who appealed to Parker. Warner, whose real name was Willard Erastus Christiansen, was from Levan, Utah. Like Roy, he had grown up in a Mormon household.

Warner's father was a Mormon bishop. According to research, Warner ran away from home in the belief he had killed another youth in a fight. Cassidy and Warner soon became fast friends. They discovered they both had a common interest—horses.

Other than drinking, gambling, and whoring, the only diversion in Telluride during those times was horseracing, which quickly became established as the main spectator sport of the area. Since Warner was earning his living at this time racing horses, he found Telluride quite to his liking. Roy, whose horsemanship skills were soon apparent to Warner, became the principal jockey.

During a horseracing event in Cortez in southeastern Colorado, Roy and Warner encountered Tom McCarty. Warner and McCarty were old friends. McCarty had married Warner's sister, making them brothers-in-law. Around this time, McCarty, who was over forty years old, had a reputation as a horse thief, cattle rustler, and gambler. Some believe he had robbed a bank only a short time before meeting Cassidy and Warner in Telluride. McCarty was wanted in at least one state. It has been written by some that McCarty, as well as Warner, had once been companions to Mike Cassidy, perhaps even members of his gang that rustled cattle. Though often stated, the relationship between Cassidy, McCarty, and Warner has never been verified to anyone's satisfaction.

Parker, McCarty, and Warner began spending a lot of time together racing horses. During the next several days they experienced a number of successes and were soon stuffing their pockets with their winnings.

As a result of a disagreement on the outcome of a horse race, the three men found themselves involved in an argument with a group of Indians. At one point during the quarrel, one of the Indians raised a rifle in a threatening gesture. McCarty responded by pulling his revolver and shooting the man, killing him instantly. The death of their companion took the fight out of the rest of the Indians, and after loading the dead man onto his horse, they rode away.

The incident, however, bothered Roy. He didn't mind a scrape now and then, but killing was something he hadn't bargained for. He didn't like it at all.

During the next few days, the three men spent most of their winnings at the Telluride taverns and were soon looking forward to the next opportunity to race. What little money they had left was given to a family of immigrants that was on the verge of starvation. Now broke, the three cast about for some opportunity to make more money. They had a difficult time drumming up horse races. Because they had been so successful, few Telluride residents were willing to take them on. After going several more days without money, they found work on a nearby ranch, but compared to the thrill and excitement of horse racing and winning purses, the three now found ranch work boring. When Parker, McCarty, and Warner finally returned to Telluride on June 22, 1889, they decided to rob the San Miguel Valley Bank.

Most historical accounts aver that, on the morning of June 24, Robert LeRoy Parker—a.k.a. Roy Parker—and Matt Warner dressed as successful businessmen and calmly strolled into the San Miguel Valley Bank. Outside, Tom McCarty held the reins to the three men's horses. A few researchers are convinced that Harry Longabaugh, a.k.a. the Sundance Kid, was somehow involved with the robbery, but his actual role, if any, is unknown and certainly undocumented. John Burroughs, the author of *Where the Old West Stayed Young*, claimed that Roy's brother, Dan, was also a participant in the robbery. In fact, Dan was later identified by a lawman as one of the robbers. A Denver newspaper that reported the robberies on June 27 stated authoritatively there were four outlaws involved.

Still others maintain a man named Bert Madden, a sometime member of the Wild Bunch, was linked to the Telluride bank robbery. Persistent research into the event reveals enough information to strongly suggest that Dan Parker, along with another man named Bert Charter, and possibly Madden, might have been associated to the degree that they helped arrange relays of fresh horses along the escape route.

Most accounts of the robbery state that Matt Warner walked up to the nearest available teller. The man looked up from his work and asked how he could be of service. In response, Warner pulled his revolver and pointed it at the man's head. As the teller raised his hands in surrender, Roy produced a sack from under his coat, walked around behind the counter, and began filling the sack with bills.

When the sack was full, the two men ran out of the front door of the bank only five minutes after entering it. By this time, however, onlookers and passersby determined a robbery had taken place. A number of citizens, following several moments of stunned silence and inaction, began shouting at the outlaws and calling for help. Quickly, the bank robbers climbed onto their mounts and, according to witnesses, leisurely rode through town heading southwest in the direction of the nearby Mancos Mountains.

After putting considerable distance between themselves and Telluride, the robbers encountered two men riding toward them. As they grew closer, the two were recognized by the bandits as acquaintances from town. Instead of stopping to greet them, however, the outlaws, concerned that a posse was not far behind, simply spurred past the pair without saying a word. Several minutes later when the two men arrived in town and were told the bank had just been robbed of $31,000, they identified Parker, Warner, and McCarty as the likely culprits. Later, it was discovered the actual amount of money taken was $20,750.

Near a location called Keystone Hill, the outlaws exchanged their weary mounts for fresh horses they had stationed there earlier. As a result of covering their tracks and setting false leads, they tricked the pursuing posse into thinking they rode in another direction. There was a total of six exchanges of horses, all likely arranged by companions for a share of the robbery money.

Now Roy Parker was officially an outlaw. In no time at all, wanted posters were out on him, McCarty, and Warner for bank robbery. The outlaws remained in hiding in the mountains for awhile, venturing now and then into small communities in the region to purchase supplies.

Most likely, the robbers remained for a time in southwestern Colorado hiding out in the mountains not far from the small town of Dolores. Some researchers are convinced this same group also robbed a train near Stoney Creek sometime during the first week of July. A search of the records indicates a train robbery did, if fact, take place, but the perpetrators were never positively identified. It is known that both McCarty and Warner had participated in at least one earlier train robbery. Some researchers suggest the two introduced young Roy Parker to the practice. After remaining in Colorado for a time, the robbers fled into Utah, convinced a Colorado posse would not pursue them into another state.

Roy Parker had over $6,500 in his saddlebags, more money than he had ever dreamed. His first thought was to send it home to his family, but he could not bring himself to pass along the ill-gotten gains to his loved ones.

When the initial thrill and excitement of the robbery finally passed, Roy was bothered deeply about his role. With his short experience thus far, living the life of an outlaw appealed very little to him—running and hiding, and seldom able to show his face in town. Roy Parker decided he wanted no more of this particular kind of adventure and was determined to lead an honest life. During his flight, his thoughts were primarily with his family and how much he missed them.

In time, Roy and his companions found themselves in Milford, Utah, just forty miles northwest of Circleville and home. Here, Roy and Dan spent some time together discussing the family. Some claim Dan arrived in Milford in the company of the robbers, but Lula Parker Betenson wrote the younger brother was living there and gainfully employed at a local business at the time.

Though Roy and Dan were close to the family and home, the former concluded that he must not return to Circleville for fear of bringing more shame and potential problems to those he loved the most. He decided to just ride away, and, with McCarty and Warner, traveled back toward the north and to Brown's Park (also known as Brown's Hole) located near the point where Utah, Colorado, and Wyoming come together. Roy knew there was work to be found on ranches and farms in the area, but more importantly, he knew that the Brown's Park region was a place where official law enforcement was virtually unknown, where a man who was wanted could hide out with little chance of being found.

Between the time the three left Milford and arrived at Brown's Park, Parker decided to change his name. He had already dropped the Robert in favor of Roy. Now, he adopted the surname of Cassidy, after Mike Cassidy, the man who had influenced him years earlier.

One afternoon, early in the summer of 1889, Robert LeRoy Parker, now known as Roy Cassidy, rode into Brown's Park and into the history books.

FOUR

Enter Butch Cassidy

Brown's Park, known to many who lived in the area as Brown's Hole, was a somewhat secluded valley approximately thirty-five miles long, six miles wide, and more or less surrounded by mountains. Brown's Park stretched from eastern Utah into western Colorado just south of the Wyoming state line. At the northern end of Brown's Park were the Cold Springs Mountains, and at the southern end were the Uinta Mountains. Within the confines of Brown's Park, the land was fertile and the graze for livestock was good. The nearby Green River provided water for irrigation, a practice established by the few farming and ranching families that lived here.

Most versions of the history of this region maintain Brown's Park was named after Baptiste Brown, a French Canadian fur trapper who came to the area during the 1820s. Brown's Park was also frequented by the famous Kit Carson during the times he earned his living as a trapper.

The rich meadows and forests of Brown's Park were once home to deer, antelope, bison, bighorn sheep, and other wildlife, but since the arrival of white settlers during the 1870s, cattle were the most dominant animals.

There is abundant evidence to suggest that, long before white immigrants came to Brown's Park, the site was home to ancient Indians. The first Anglo arrivals to this area reported finding long abandoned and undisturbed Indian campsites. Even today numerous petroglyphs and pictographs dating from prehistoric America can be found on canyon walls.

The residents of Brown's Park were aware of the occasional presence of outlaws who used the area as a hiding place. Since they were never harmed and were, in fact, often aided by the outlaws, their reactions to them ranged from reserved tolerance to overt friendship. Many of the nearby ranchers often hired the outlaws to work for them.

John Burroughs writes that the outlaws appeared from time to time at homesteads requesting a meal or fresh horses. Generally, they were accommodated, and the homesteaders were, more often than not, paid handsomely for their help. As a result, many of the homesteaders refused to cooperate with lawmen who arrived in Brown's Park in search of criminals.

Deep within Brown's Park near Diamond Mountain at the southeastern end was an abandoned cabin. Here many of the outlaws congregated on arriving in the region.

Soon after coming to Brown's Park, Robert LeRoy Parker, a.k.a. Roy Parker, a.k.a. Roy Cassidy, changed his name once again, this time to George Cassidy. One of the first people he met when he rode into Brown's Park in 1890 was a rancher and freighter named Charley Crouse. Crouse was a friend to many of the outlaws who frequented the park and was often rewarded for warning them of approaching lawmen. Crouse let Cassidy, Matt Warner, and Tom McCarty use the abandoned cabin located near Diamond Mountain and introduced them to area residents.

After asking around, Cassidy learned there was an opening for a cowhand at the Bassett Ranch. Herb and Elizabeth (sometimes referred to as Mary) Bassett were originally from Arkansas. Herb had worked as a court clerk in Arkansas but lost his job when a new political party was elected into office. Taking his wife and five children, he headed west in search of work. Initially, Herb Bassett was infused with the notion that his future lay in California. Some researchers claim that Bassett moved west because he suffered from asthma. He was indeed an asthma victim—he suffered badly and often. Bassett may also have had malaria, and the damp Arkansas climate no doubt aggravated his condition. While Bassett anticipated that relocating in the American West would likely be good for his health, it has been concluded that his primary reasons for the move were economic rather than health related.

The Bassett family stopped in Brown's Park to visit Herb's brother, Sam. Sam had been to California and did not have many positive things to relate to Herb about his experiences there. Instead, Sam convinced his brother to remain in Brown's Park and take up ranching and farming.

Cassidy took an instant liking to the Bassett family, in part because they reminded him of his own. Herb Bassett was well educated and kept an extensive library. Cassidy loved to read and was often invited by Herb to help himself to books. According to author Gail Drago, Cassidy liked to read "Scottish history, Dickens, and medieval literature."

George Cassidy easily fit into the scheme of things on the Bassett Ranch and proved to be a top hand. When he wasn't performing chores, he spent time with the Bassett couple and their children. On social occasions when neighbors were invited over for dinner, dancing, and games, Cassidy was always asked to participate. He endeared himself to the neighboring ranchers, often offering to help them out with their work or playing with their children.

Cassidy soon became close friends with two of Bassett's daughters—Ann and Josie. One of them, Josephine, or Josie, as she was called, remained Cassidy's close friend throughout his life. It is believed by some that the two were lovers. She was fifteen years old at the time.

Many of the Brown's Park females were attracted to Cassidy. He was always polite and gentlemanly, loved to dance, and only drank in moderation. In turn, Cassidy was attracted to many of the women he met, often invited them to dances, and was known to court several.

It was probably at the Bassett Ranch that Cassidy met Elzy Lay. Full name William Ellsworth Lay, Elzy had come to the West looking for work. Some accounts claim Lay was from Texas, others insist his home was Illinois or Iowa, and a few maintain he was from Boston. Author Richard Patterson believes Lay was born November 25, 1868, in or near McArthur, Ohio, a time and place ascribed to by most Cassidy scholars.

Lay has been described as tall, slim, handsome (with light brown hair and round hazel eyes), and exceptionally well mannered. Those who knew him regarded him as kindly, polite, and gentlemanly. Lay often went by the alias William McGinnis, which was actually the name of one of his boyhood friends. Some researchers believe that Lay's real name was, in fact, McGinnis but have yet to provide evidence of this. During his time as an active outlaw, Lay was involved with cattle rustling, horse theft, robbery, operating a gambling den, and counterfeiting.

Cassidy and Lay proved to have much in common, and the two were about the same age. Both loved horses and working with riding stock, and like Cassidy, Lay proved himself to be a skilled horseman. He soon found employment breaking horses for Herb Bassett.

It was inevitable that Cassidy and Lay would become good friends. While they worked at the Bassett Ranch they were almost inseparable.

They broke and trained horses together, and occasionally roped and branded mavericks.

As a result of William Goldman's extremely popular film *Butch Cassidy and the Sundance Kid*, as well as a variety of interpretations by well-intentioned but careless researchers and writers, a man named Harry Longabaugh, alias the Sundance Kid, is often represented as the boon companion to Cassidy. While it is clear that Cassidy and Longabaugh spent several years together in various adventures in South America, the charismatic outlaw actually spent most of his time with Elzy Lay and considered him his best friend.

In search of a better paying job, George Cassidy eventually quit the Bassett Ranch and traveled to Rock Springs, Wyoming, about seventy miles to the north. On arriving at this bustling town, he learned that the only jobs available were in the coal mines. Having had enough of mine-associated work, he determined to find something else.

While he was hanging around town hoping to land work, Cassidy met a man named William Gottsche. Gottsche owned a butcher shop and, as it happened, was looking for a helper. Robert LeRoy Parker introduced himself to the butcher as Ed Cassidy, inquired about the job, and was hired immediately.

Cassidy enjoyed working in Gottsche's butcher shop, and before long he was known by virtually everyone in town. He was described as charming and friendly, always smiling, and he was known to give the customers a bit more meat than they paid for.

In a very short time, according to a number of Cassidy historians, customers of Gottsche's meat market were referring to him as Butcher Cassidy. This was soon shortened to "Butch," and thereafter the charming young man with the winning ways was known as Butch Cassidy. Though many ascribe to this version of how Cassidy got his nickname, the story is likely apocryphal.

Another version of how Cassidy received his nickname comes from author Larry Pointer. He writes that a man named Joe Gras was told that Cassidy was given the name "Butch" while working in a meat market owned by Otto Schnauber.

In his book, Matt Warner claims he was responsible for giving Cassidy his nickname. According to Warner, he lent Cassidy his needle gun, which was named "Butch." On his initial attempt at firing the gun, Cassidy was knocked on his back. Thereafter, wrote Warner, Cassidy was known as "Butch."

There is yet another explanation for the origin of the nickname. Cowboys who worked roundups and were responsible for providing meat for the camp cook pot were nicknamed "butches." With Cassidy, some sources claim, this name apparently stuck.

Some researchers have contended that, while Cassidy was working for Gottsche, he was also stealing cattle in the area and selling them on the sly to the butcher. Nothing definite, however, has ever been found to substantiate this notion.

The name Cassidy, at least the spelling of it, is also a bit controversial. There is evidence that Butch actually spelled the surname "Casidy" prior to 1893, and perhaps even inscribed it as such on a wooden grip of one of his pistols.

Butch Cassidy endeared himself to Rock Springs residents in other ways. A story is told that one evening, while enjoying a leisurely drink in one of the town's taverns, another customer, a lawyer named Douglas A. Preston, became involved in an argument with an irate patron. When it became clear that the patron intended to kill Preston, Cassidy stepped in, diffused the situation, and, according to researchers, very likely saved the lawyer's life. Cassidy and Preston eventually became good friends. In the not too distant future, lawyer Preston would represent Cassidy, as well as a few of his friends, on several different occasions in court.

In another somewhat dramatic incident that allegedly took place in Rock Springs, Butch Cassidy is credited with saving the life of the town marshal, Harry S. Parker. As Cassidy was cutting meat in the butcher shop one afternoon, a group of Finnish coal miners had grown drunk and troublesome in a nearby gambling hall. After the Finns had threatened customers and broken furniture, the owner of the hall summoned the marshal. Minutes later, Cassidy watched from the butcher shop window as Marshal Parker entered the saloon and confronted the rowdy Finns.

From the shouting and cursing that emanated from the gambling hall, Cassidy realized that the Finns were determined to kill Parker. Grabbing a large meat cleaver, he left the butcher shop and entered the establishment. Inside, the Finns closed in on Parker with knives, broken beer bottles, and clubs. Cassidy, brandishing the cleaver, shouted a warning and the Finns paused to regard the newcomer. At that instant, a Union Pacific guard walked in carrying a rifle and pointed it at the unruly men. Following a few seconds of silent confrontation, the Finns backed away and Parker was spirited out of the hall.

Butch Cassidy's run of good luck in Rock Springs was about to come to an end through no fault of his own. He was soon to encounter another experience that would leave him bitter and disappointed with the law.

One evening after dinner Butch went to a local saloon for a few drinks and some conversation. He soon found himself visiting with an acquaintance, a man who was unable to hold his liquor. Following a few drinks, Butch's companion was hopelessly inebriated, spilling his drinks, and dropping his money onto the bar and the floor. Butch decided he had had enough of the man's company, paid for his drinks, and left the saloon.

After Butch left, the owner of the saloon, who was also serving as bartender, had his eye on the spilled money. When the drunken customer looked in another direction, the owner surreptitiously picked up the coins and placed them in his own pocket. Among the coins, it has been related, were several twenty-dollar gold pieces.

The following day, the drunkard returned to the saloon and accused the bartender of stealing his money. The bartender allegedly told the man he had seen Butch Cassidy take the coins, and even provided several witnesses to testify so. Cassidy was subsequently arrested for and charged with the theft.

Though nothing came of the charge, Cassidy was thereafter discouraged with the way the legal system worked. Lula Parker Betenson stated that her brother strongly believed the laws were intended to "protect people and their rights," but he soon came to realize that the same laws more often than not served to protect and aid those who already had money and power.

With growing bitterness, Butch Cassidy recalled how years earlier a portion of his own family's homestead was given to someone else who had no legal or moral right to the land. He also remembered instances where small homesteaders had to give way to the wishes of the moneyed and powerful. Soon, he began to notice how banks and railroad companies, using the legal system they manipulated, took land from those who were too poor to afford to put up any kind of fight. Butch's rancor against the wealthy and powerful deepened. During those times when Cassidy grew depressed and discouraged about such things, he returned to Brown's Park, where he was always welcomed.

Butch Cassidy gradually became determined that he was not going to be pushed around by those who tended to abuse their power and office. Many of Butch's friends felt the same way, and in time these companions who thought and acted alike banded together and often discussed ways in which they might thwart the influence of the powerful corporations and landholders. They gradually moved out of town and often camped together in the foothills of the nearby mountains. Residents of the area began referring to them as "that wild bunch from Brown's Park." Cassidy and his companions eventually became known throughout the region as the Wild Bunch.

According to writer Burroughs, the Wild Bunch was "wild without other purpose or direction than that dictated by the whim of the moment, their appetites, or their sense of humor." In truth, they were a generally good-natured group of ne'er-do-wells who occasionally gambled, drank, and stole horses and cattle from time to time.

In spite of the "gang" appellation, Butch Cassidy and his friends, though mostly mischievous and boisterous and certainly not beyond rustling livestock from a big rancher, were neither malicious nor violent. On occasion, Cassidy helped out ranchers who couldn't afford to hire hands, helped them pay their taxes, bought Christmas presents for children, chopped wood and carried water for widows, and helped many a starving rancher pay off his mortgage. A statement often attributed to Josie Bassett was that "Butch took care of more poor people than FDR, and with no red tape."

Stories emerged from time to time about cattle being stolen from some of the large herds in the vicinity, and though most suspected the Wild Bunch, no evidence ever surfaced linking them to the thefts. From time to time following a major cattle theft, the Wild Bunch would ride into Rock Springs and spend the evening drinking in one of the saloons and spending money freely.

This nucleus of rustlers and, in some cases, mostly idealistic young men would eventually grow into one of the most feared gangs of train and bank robbers in the United States. Most of them would be wanted for their crimes throughout much of the American West.

FIVE

Prison

During the early 1890s, an incident took place that reinforced and solidified Butch Cassidy's attitudes toward wealth, power, and the law, and placed his feet firmly on the outlaw trail.

Around 1890, Cassidy took a job with the EA Ranch in west-central Wyoming's Wind River country between the town of Lander and the Wind River. The owner was Eugenio Amoretti, an Italian immigrant. Needing men to take care of his immense herd of cattle—over forty thousand—Amoretti hired, among others, Butch Cassidy. Amoretti and Cassidy would become good friends during the ensuing years.

At about the same time Cassidy went to work for the EA outfit, Amoretti hired another young man named Al Hainer (sometimes spelled Hainey). As with Elzy Lay, Butch and Al became good friends and, at one point, in 1891 or 1892, they decided to file together for a homestead at Horse Creek near the Wind River in Fremont County. Here, the two friends constructed a log cabin on the banks of the creek and gradually established a fine herd of horses.

While Cassidy and Hainer were living on the homestead, Deputy Sheriff Bob Caverly noted that the two men were often seen selling horses but were never known to purchase any. Suspecting they were stealing their stock, Caverly kept an eye on the newcomers. In spite of his efforts, he was never able to prove anything.

Because of his gregarious ways and his obvious and occasionally marketable skills with livestock, Butch became well known to most of the Wind River area ranchers and residents. Popular with the neighbors, he was often invited to dances and other gatherings at various homes throughout the region. As in Brown's Park, Butch grew to like his neighbors and proved himself to be a good neighbor as well.

During the extremely cold and brutal winter of 1892–1893, ranching in the Wind River region came to a near standstill. To compound the problems, a severe flu epidemic spread across the region, striking down normally strong and healthy men and rendering them bedridden. On those occasions when Butch heard of a neighbor who was too sick to work, he would travel to the ranch and perform necessary chores, generally remaining until the sickness passed and the rancher was able to return to his work.

John and Margaret Simpson were Cassidy's neighbors. Margaret often treated sick neighbors with her concoctions of herbal medicines. When the weather was so bad that Margaret was unable to deliver her medicines, Butch carried them to those who needed them the worst. Margaret Simpson once stated that Butch Cassidy "saved more than one life" as a result of his efforts. According to Lula Parker Betenson, "When [Butch] was around, the water buckets were always full and the wood box running over."

While Butch proved himself a valuable member of the Wind River community, he continued to ride with the Wild Bunch as well as rustle cattle and steal horses from the wealthy and powerful.

Wyoming resident Ada Calvert was a young girl when Butch Cassidy lived in that part of the country. She once recalled that he was a boisterous sort of lad but always good-natured and good-humored. She also stated that, when members of the Wild Bunch got out of control, it was always Butch who talked to them and set them straight.

Once, near Baggs, Wyoming, located close to the Colorado border, Butch and the Wild Bunch stole thirty horses belonging to Kirk Calvert, Ada's father. One of Ada's brothers started to raise a posse to go after the horse thieves, but Calvert talked them out of it. Months later, Calvert received payment for the horses from Butch Cassidy.

While working and rustling his way around Wyoming and Colorado, the always charming Butch Cassidy remained a favorite of the young girls. He loved to dance and court the women. According to all accounts he always remained a gentleman, always courteous and always considerate.

A woman named Dora Lamorreaux was very close to Cassidy during this time. Those who knew the couple were convinced the two were quite serious about one another, and most believed they intended to marry. Rarely were they seen apart except when Cassidy was performing his chores. During his free time, the two often went horseback riding, dancing, and even to church. Lamorreaux characterized Cassidy as a "gentleman."

Apparently unable to find comfort with just one woman, Cassidy also courted and became good friends with the half-Indian Mary Boyd around the same time he was squiring Dora Lamorreaux. Researchers suggest that Butch became enamored of Boyd, even more than he was of Lamorreaux, and may even have expressed a desire to marry her and settle down. According to Boyd's granddaughter, Ione Manning, as reported by Larry Pointer, Mary may have actually lived with Cassidy for a time. In 1892, Boyd gave birth to a daughter, a child who was conceived in August 1891.

Some Cassidy researchers contend that the baby was Cassidy's, but substantial evidence is lacking. Around the time of the birth, Cassidy was arrested for horse theft. As Mary was an unwed mother, the baby was eventually given to Boyd's Indian relatives and named Mary B'Hat. When she was older, Mary B'Hat was told by her relatives that her father was a Lander businessman her mother "became infatuated with." Mary Boyd subsequently married O. E. Rhodes, a Lander cowboy, while Butch Cassidy was serving a prison term in the Wyoming State Penitentiary.

The Wild Bunch found the pickings good in the southern Wyoming and northern Colorado region, and during the next several months a lot of horses and cattle were discovered missing from the large ranches in the area.

Though he stole livestock with impunity, Butch was not insensitive to the misfortune and misery of others. Once, when the Little Snake River flooded and jeopardized Calvert's store at Baggs, Butch and several members of the Wild Bunch forded the swift current and offered their help.

Though he spent a good deal of time stealing livestock, Butch Cassidy is seldom identified as a rustler—more often he was credited with being a bank and train robber. The banks and trains were to come later; most of Cassidy's formative outlaw years were spent stealing cattle and horses from the large corporate ranches. Several of the ranchers attempted to hire Cassidy. Even though he possessed a growing reputation as a rustler, it was well known that he would never steal from an employer. Most of the ranchers were convinced they would rather have Cassidy working for them than against them.

Some have considered that Cassidy's rustling was done more out of amusement and boyish devilment as opposed to pure malicious intent. Perhaps Butch Cassidy felt he was exacting some sort of revenge on the moneyed and powerful. For every misdeed he was involved with, however, someone had something good to say about Cassidy when it came to helping out his fellow man.

It was inevitable that Butch Cassidy would eventually be caught. During August 1891, Cassidy, most likely accompanied by Al Hainer, was residing at a location called Mail Camp in Fremont County, Wyoming, when a young man named Billy Nutcher rode in with a string of three saddle horses—a brown, a grey, and a sorrel. When Cassidy inquired, Nutcher said the horses were for sale, and the two dickered over a price for a time. Eventually, Cassidy bought all three, and the two shook hands on the deal. Unfortunately for Cassidy, none of the appropriate paperwork for the three horses was provided.

As it turned out, Billy Nutcher, like Butch Cassidy, was a horse thief, and the three mounts he sold had recently been stolen by him from the nearby Grey Bull Cattle Company. After Cassidy had been reported in possession of the stolen stock, Deputy Sheriff Caverly went after him. According to writer John Rolfe Burroughs (*Where the Old West Stayed Young*), on April 8, 1892, some ten months after the transaction, Caverly finally overtook Cassidy, and the two allegedly engaged in a brief gunfight. There exist a variety of versions about what transpired. According to an article in the *Fremont Clipper* on April 15, 1892, Cassidy refused to be arrested. At that point, Caverly "grappled with him and after a desperate struggle in which the desperado was beaten senseless, and the cuffs and shackles were applied to his limbs, he was conveyed to the prison at Evanston."

In the June 16, 1939, issue of the *Wyoming State Tribune*, a letter written by Caverly was published in which he described the confrontation with Cassidy. Caverly wrote that, after he informed the outlaw he had a warrant for his arrest, Cassidy suggested they "get to shooting," and the two men pulled their guns. According to John Rolfe Burroughs, Caverly said he placed "the barrel of my revolver almost to his stomach, but it missed three times but owing to the fact that there was another man between us, he failed to hit me. The fourth time I snapped the gun it went off and the bullet hit him in the upper part of the forehead and felled him."

Ultimately, the result was that Cassidy was grazed in the head by a bullet and rendered unconscious. By the time he regained his senses, he had been handcuffed and formally arrested.

On July 15, 1892 (some sources say July 16), Butch Cassidy and Al Hainer were both charged with stealing a horse valued at forty dollars. They pled not guilty and were placed in jail, with Butch being booked under the name George Cassidy. A short time later, the two men hired lawyers Douglas A. Preston and C. E. Rathbone to defend them.

Cassidy and Hainer were subsequently released on a $400 bond and appeared in court in June of the following year. On June 22, 1893, both men were found not guilty of the crime of horse theft. On June 19, however, another charge of stealing a horse was filed against Cassidy and Hainer. The complaint charged the two with stealing a horse from a Richard Ashworth (sometimes reported as Ainsworth) two years earlier. Ashworth, who was from Great Britain, was the owner of the Grey Bull Cattle Company. Cassidy's friend, Douglas Preston, served as an attorney for the defense once again.

On July 4, 1894, a verdict was delivered that found Butch Cassidy "guilty of horse stealing, as charged in the information, and we find the value of the property stolen to be $5.00." Al Hainer was found not guilty. Attorney Preston filed an appeal, but it was denied. Cassidy was subsequently sentenced on July 10 by Judge Jesse Knight to serve two years of hard labor at the Wyoming State Penitentiary at Laramie. The maximum penalty was ten years.

Following the sentencing, Cassidy and Hainer separated, never to be reunited. After having time to consider the circumstances of his sentencing, Cassidy eventually became convinced that Hainer bargained with the court, providing, or perhaps manufacturing, evidence that led to the guilty verdict in return for his freedom. Cassidy also ultimately came to believe he had been set up by the cattle barons and that Hainer was involved in the plot.

Butch Cassidy was delivered by Fremont County sheriff Charles Stough to the prison on July 15 in the back of an open wagon along with five other men. Stough was accompanied by his deputy Harry Logue and Lander constable Henry Boedeker. Cassidy was the only prisoner who was not shackled, and when a prison official asked why, Boedeker explained that Cassidy was the only one who could be trusted not to escape.

He was admitted into the prison as George "Butch" Cassidy, convict number 187. Over the years biographers, using only prison records, have often applied the first name "George" to the famous outlaw, either claiming or suggesting it was his real first name. Not wishing to visit the shame and embarrassment of his misdeeds and sentencing onto his family, Cassidy found it easy to lie to prison officials about his name when his admission form was filled out. He also told them he was from New York City, that his parents were unknown, that he did not know the whereabouts of any living relatives, and that he had no religion. He was listed as being five feet nine inches in height.

In prison, Cassidy was well behaved and worked hard. He had several opportunities to participate in escape attempts but declined. The notion has been advanced that Cassidy learned a lot about criminal activity while imprisoned. Although he was a convicted horse thief, he was incarcerated with a number of others who were serving time for horse and cattle rustling. Furthermore, it has been suspected that fellow inmate John Worley, a former railroad employee, schooled Cassidy in the rudiments of train robbery.

Ironically, another of Cassidy's fellow prisoners was Billy Nutcher, the young man who "sold" Cassidy the very horse he was charged with stealing. Nutcher was also serving time for horse theft.

Cassidy proved to be no trouble whatsoever to prison authorities, and after eighteen months he was called before Wyoming governor W. A. Richards to discuss an early release. The following story may be apocryphal, but according to writer Betenson, the governor confessed to being under some pressure from some of the state's leading cattlemen—they were not looking forward to the day Cassidy was released from prison. They feared that a man with his leadership abilities as well as his penchant for and success in rustling cattle boded ill for the future. The governor, apparently at the urging of several ranchers, agreed to release Cassidy early if the outlaw would consent to not ever bother Wyoming's cattlemen again.

Cassidy readily agreed to the proposition. When Richards asked him why he was so willing to make such a bargain, Cassidy allegedly told him straightforwardly that cattle and horse theft was "just too slow a way to get rich." He told the governor that when you need money, you should go where it is. When the governor inquired of the soon-to-be released prisoner where that would be, Cassidy reportedly replied, "In banks." Before the interview was over, however, the clearly concerned Richards exacted a promise from Cassidy that, in addition to Wyoming's cattlemen, he would leave the banks alone, too.

Butch Cassidy was officially pardoned on January 19, 1896. As he rode away from Laramie, he pointed his mount in the direction of Brown's Park. The long journey gave him time to think, and the more he thought about his previous year and a half in prison and the circumstances that led to it, the angrier he became.

Cassidy was convinced that his prison sentence was the result of a conspiracy to get him off the range. While he had certainly taken horses and cattle, the ultimate conviction and sentence had been based on what he considered a made-up charge over a five-dollar horse. Once again, he was certain, it was a case of the powerful and wealthy manipulating the laws to place those with lesser means at a disadvantage.

Butch Cassidy's time for revenge would come.

SIX

Robberies

Over the years there has been discussion among researchers as to when Butch Cassidy actually became committed to pursuing the life of an outlaw and the reasons behind the decision. While many of his earlier illegal escapades may have resulted from some level of roguish or prankish behavior, many believe his eighteen-month-long prison sentence oriented him toward the bad, the experience turning him into a hardened outlaw.

Others—those who lean more toward ascribing a certain idealism and a Robin Hood image to Cassidy—maintain there were altruistic reasons for his outlaw adventures, that he perceived the existence of an imbalance of justice in the world between corporate powers and the small rancher who toiled to make a living. Still others suggest his outlawry was simply a kind of revenge against established authority, by whom he, Cassidy, himself had been affected. His retaliation against existing powers, some have speculated, was simply Cassidy's method of making a statement to the effect that the common man was not going to lay down and allow the rich and powerful to run over him.

Regardless of his motives, real or suspected, Butch Cassidy turned to bank robberies with a certain zeal heretofore not applied to his misdeeds, and he accomplished these, as well as other crimes, with a style and competence heretofore unknown in the history of American outlawry.

Shortly after returning to Brown's Park, Cassidy renewed his friendship with Matt Warner and Elzy Lay. By this time, Warner had married Rose Morgan, the eighteen-year-old daughter of a Star Valley Mormon family. Not long after giving birth to their daughter, Hayda, Rose was diagnosed with cancer. In order to receive proper treatment, she moved to Vernal, Utah, while Warner held down a job in Brown's

Park. Warner and Lay shared a cabin, and shortly after arriving in the area, Cassidy moved in with them.

Sometime during 1896, Warner was hired by E. B. Coleman and Bob Swift to keep trespassers and potential claim jumpers and thieves away from their gold mining enterprise in the Uinta Mountains. Like Coleman and Swift, a trio of prospectors—Dave Milton, Dick Staunton, and Ike Staunton—was trying to locate the source of a rich mineral deposit. One afternoon, Milton and the Stauntons entered Coleman's property and a brief gunfight resulted. By the time it was over, Milton and Dick Staunton were dead. Warner, Coleman, and another man named Bill Wall were arrested, charged with murder, and placed in the Vernal, Utah, jail.

Rumors soon spread through town that Butch Cassidy and Elzy Lay were going to break Warner out of jail. Whether this was true or not, no one knows, but the fact remains that the two men showed up in Vernal a few days later. While in town, Cassidy received a message from Warner that he was desperately in need of money to hire a defense lawyer.

In the meantime, several Vernal residents, outraged at what they considered the wanton killings of Milton and Staunton, threatened to break into the jail, remove the prisoners, and hang them from the nearest tree.

Concerned about the possibility of a lynch mob, or perhaps, as some researchers maintain, that Cassidy and Lay might attempt to break the prisoners out of their cell, the authorities transferred Warner and Wall to the jail at Ogden, Utah, to await trial. Ogden was located 140 miles in a direct line to the northwest.

On learning of the circumstances of Warner's arrest, Cassidy and Lay were convinced their friend killed only in self-defense. The two immediately turned to lawyer Douglas A. Preston and asked him to represent their companion. Preston agreed and informed Cassidy and Lay that the trial could be long and involved and that his fee would be substantial. The two friends told Preston to begin his preparations and that they would make certain he was paid. According to Lula Parker Betenson, in order to come up with the money to pay Preston, Cassidy and Lay decided to rob the bank in Montpelier, Idaho.

Montpelier was a small town located in the southeastern corner of Idaho and about one hundred miles northeast of Ogden. Originally settled by Mormons in 1865, it was supposedly named after the Vermont birthplace of church leader Brigham Young. In truth, Young was born in Wittingham, Vermont.

The subsequent location of a railroad line through the town of Montpelier brought a number of non-Mormon laborers into the area. The town, located on the side of the tracks opposite the Mormon settlement, was similar to most new and rapidly growing towns of the time in this region—saloons, gambling dens, and dance halls provided a stark contrast to the conservative religious community nearby. The growing numbers of miners, trappers, hunters, gamblers, and drummers, along with their wild ways, troubled and angered the Mormons. Tensions remained high for a time. To make things worse, the railroad eventually brought in federal authorities to enforce monogamy laws on the polygamous Mormons. Soon, Montpelier teemed with saloons, mercantiles, and dance halls. It also had a bank.

During this time Butch Cassidy established a pattern for robbery that, with some few exceptions, he was to follow throughout most of the rest of his outlaw career. Several days prior to a holdup, whether bank or train, Cassidy and his gang would arrive early and study the work schedules, the comings and goings of employees, and generally become acquainted with the personnel and their habits. Furthermore, they cached food and fresh mounts at strategic locations along the escape route, thus ensuring they would easily outdistance pursuing posses, most of which were hastily assembled and poorly equipped. During subsequent train robberies, dynamite was often employed to open up locked payroll cars and safes.

During the first week of August, Butch Cassidy, Elzy Lay, and a friend named Bub Meeks (sometimes reported as Bob Meeks) arrived in the Montpelier area and found work cutting hay at a nearby ranch. When the opportunity arose, the three rode into town and familiarized themselves with the hours and operations of the bank. Like Cassidy and Lay, Meeks was another wayward Mormon.

A few minutes past three o'clock on the afternoon of August 13, 1896, Cassidy, Lay, and Meeks rode into Montpelier and reined their horses up in front of the town's only bank. As Meeks held the horses, Cassidy and Lay, pulling bandanas over their faces and drawing revolvers, entered the financial establishment. Once inside, they noted a pair of cashiers and three or four customers. Hardly pausing, the two men announced that a robbery was about to take place and ordered everyone to raise their hands and place their faces against a nearby wall.

Some writers insist Meeks led the three mounts to the rear of the bank, while others are just as certain he remained near the front entrance.

According to author Pat Wilde, an assistant cashier named A. M. "Bud" McIntosh observed a man holding horses at the front of the bank while the robbery was in progress.

Cassidy stood near the front door and guarded the customers as Lay, pulling a canvas sack from his belt, walked behind the cashier's cage and ordered McIntosh to place all of the bills into the sack. McIntosh told the robber there wasn't any currency. In response, Lay called him a liar and struck him across the forehead with the barrel of his revolver. Cassidy, witnessing the incident, admonished Lay and told him not to hurt anyone. Bleeding from his wound, McIntosh emptied the bills out of his cash drawer and passed them to Lay who, in turn, stuffed them into the sack. Lay then walked into the open vault, grabbed more currency, and added it to the rest. As he prepared to return to the front of the bank, he spotted some gold coins behind the counter and hurriedly scooped them into a cloth bank bag he found nearby. After adding a few silver coins he found on McIntosh's counter, he rejoined Cassidy near the door.

While Cassidy held his gun on the customers, Lay walked out, tied the loot to his saddles, and mounted up. Cassidy then backed out, warning those inside not to move for ten minutes.

Once outside, Cassidy vaulted onto his mount. The three outlaws rode slowly out of town trying not to arouse suspicion. Once they passed beyond the town's limits, they spurred their horses into a gallop and fled northeast toward Montpelier Canyon. A deputy sheriff named Fred Cruickshank jumped on a bicycle and gave chase but was easily outdistanced by the robbers.

Within an hour of the holdup, a somewhat unwilling posse was formed and set out in pursuit of the outlaws. In Montpelier Canyon, Cassidy, Lay, and Meeks switched to different horses they had hidden nearby the previous day. With fresh mounts, the trio quickly outdistanced the pursuing posse, which eventually gave up and returned to town.

The following day, Cassidy, Lay, and Meeks counted the take and discovered they were considerably richer. Estimates of the robbery loot range from $7,000 to more than $30,000, with most researchers leaning toward the higher amount. The outlaws then split up. Cassidy and Lay rode straight to Douglas Preston's office in Rock Springs and paid him a handsome advance to defend Matt Warner. Preston, a Wyoming lawyer, was not allowed to practice in Utah, so he hired two able attorneys from that state—D. N. Straupp and Orlando W. Powers.

According to legend, Butch Cassidy buried some or all of his share of the Montpelier bank loot somewhere in the Wind River Mountains. The most commonly related version of the story maintains the outlaw dug a shallow hole in some sand with the butt of his pistol, deposited the money, and covered it up. Nearby was a lightning-struck stump to which he could refer as a landmark. Several years later when the tale of outlaw-buried loot spread throughout the region, treasure hunters and hikers came to the Wind River Mountains in search of this lightning-struck stump in hopes of finding the buried loot.

Charges immediately surfaced that Preston had received payment from bank robbery money. He steadfastly denied it, claiming he had been provided an advance by friends of Warner long before the Montpelier bank was robbed. He further maintained he was not retained by Cassidy or any of his gang members.

Despite the efforts of Preston, Warner was ultimately convicted of the killing and sentenced to a five-year term in the Utah State Penitentiary. While Warner was incarcerated, Cassidy often visited his wife and provided her with money until her husband was finally freed. Meeks was arrested a short time later, tried, convicted, and sentenced to prison for thirty-five years.

With the passage of a few months, Butch Cassidy began hanging out with a group of outlaws called the Hole-in-the-Wall Gang. From time to time, these men were involved in a variety of criminal activities, and it is believed Cassidy participated in many of them.

The Hole in the Wall was a well-known hideout for outlaws in central Wyoming and was located along the eastern slope of the Rocky Mountains some sixty miles northwest of Casper. According to writer Gail Drago, the Hole in the Wall consisted, in part, of a "great cliff of red rock, a red wall composed of a fifty-mile sandstone ridge . . . divided only by a narrow, twisting V-shaped notch, barely wide enough for a man on horseback. The entrance to the Hole in the Wall could be easily guarded. With little difficulty, a man armed with a rifle could pick off a rider slowly making his way up the narrow, winding trail."

The Hole in the Wall was, and still is, not a hole at all but a V-shaped notch in a high canyon rim. Even today, this region remains somewhat remote and isolated. It was these same geographic characteristics, however, that provided sanctuary to rustlers, robbers, and killers whose presence was more or less tolerated by the few ranchers and farmers scattered throughout the region. The Hole in the Wall has sometimes been referred to as the northernmost point along the so-called Outlaw Trail.

Researchers generally agree that Butch Cassidy grew to be the acknowledged leader of the Hole-in-the-Wall Gang, although the position was entirely informal. Occasionally, Harvey "Kid Curry" Logan served as leader, but more often than not he deferred to Cassidy when the latter was present. Cassidy, say some historians, apparently possessed natural leadership skills and appeared to get along well with practically everyone. Evidence suggests that, during the time Cassidy was in prison, the gang conducted its outlawry in a loose, careless, often bungling, and clearly leaderless manner.

According to most who have studied the Hole-in-the-Wall Gang, it was considered a loose-knit and often changing association of bad men. On various occasions Dave Atkins, Will Carver, Nate Champion, Bill Cruzan, Pegleg Elliot, O. C. "Deaf Charlie" Hanks, Ben Kilpatrick, Elzy Lay, Bob Lee, Harry Longabaugh (the Sundance Kid), Tom McCarty, Bob Meeks, Tom O'Day, Walt Punteney, Will Roberts, and Harry Tracy were members of the gang.

During this period Cassidy met Harry Longabaugh, who eventually gained a level of outlaw fame as the Sundance Kid. Longabaugh, originally from Pennsylvania, had recently arrived in the area and joined the gang of outlaws. Almost all of Longabaugh's biographers refer to him as tall and handsome, and he was known to dress well and in the latest styles. A successful gambler, Longabaugh was also a skilled pistoleer. He was known to have killed men with his handguns. He was also a very talented horseman. These attributes, along with his short temper and latent meanness, did little to prevent him from fitting in with the rest of the outlaws.

For the most part, the Hole-in-the-Wall Gang hid out at Robber's Roost. In Matt Warner's autobiography, he described Robber's Roost as "wild country. . . . The wildest kind of buttes and spires rise above the level of the mesas . . . deep, dizzy canyons." Newspapers reported the streams held treacherous quicksand.

Warner wrote that a number of outlaws knew the advantages of hiding out at Robber's Roost, a remote, mazelike canyon land located in southeastern Utah, roughly between Hanksville to the west and Moab to the east. There were a number of cabins in the Roost, as well as plenty of freshwater springs and graze for the horses.

It was extremely difficult to track men on the run in that rough country. Many lawmen avoided the Roost for they were simply not willing to encounter desperate outlaws in their own, easily defensible territory.

Over the years, outlaws on the run—the Hole-in-the-Wall Gang as well as others—hid out in a number of different locations in Wayne County, Utah, west of the Green River; all of the locations at one time or another were referred to as "Robber's Roost."

In 1896, Elzy Lay married Maude Davis. The two moved to Robber's Roost and lived in a tent during the winter months. Nearby, living in another tent, were Harry Longabaugh and his woman, Etta Place.

While many researchers and writers are in agreement that Etta Place and Longabaugh were lovers, it has been speculated that she may have actually been Butch Cassidy's woman, at least for a short time. In the book *The Wild Bunch at Robber's Roost* by Pearl Baker, the author claims Etta Place and Butch Cassidy shared a tent. Still other researchers maintain there is no substantial evidence that the woman living in the tent with the Sundance Kid (or Butch Cassidy) at the time was Etta Place. Even today, Etta Place remains one of the American West's most mysterious and enigmatic figures.

Sometime in the spring of 1897, the gang disbanded for a time and all moved out of Robber's Roost. Before leaving the hideaway, however, Cassidy and Lay concocted plans to rob the payroll from the Pleasant Valley Coal Company (PVCC) at Castle Gate, Utah.

Castle Gate was located in the northeastern part of the state near Price. The town had little reason to exist save for coal. Coal mining and associated businesses dominated the economics of Castle Gate, almost to the exclusion of all others. Buildings, roads, and most of the residents of the town seemed to be perpetually covered in coal dust.

This was the setting when Butch Cassidy and Elzy Lay rode into the town. Some claim they were accompanied by Bub Meeks and Joe Walker, but there is no clear consensus on this.

Cassidy and Lay worked for a short time at a nearby ranch, coming into town occasionally to investigate procedures relative to the arrival and disbursement of the payroll. Since Castle Gate was overwhelmingly a mining town, the arrival of two cowhands on horseback was a noteworthy event and attracted attention. Because attention was the last thing they wished, and because they were determined to learn the somewhat irregular and confusing payroll schedule, Cassidy and Lay decided they needed to do something that would allow them to come and go without arousing suspicion. They quickly learned that, while there were few horses in Castle Gate, horse racing was a popular activity. Fitting their mounts with racing saddles and bridles, they told anyone who inquired that they were training their horses for upcoming races in Salt Lake City. This response appeared to satisfy the curious.

The two outlaws soon learned that the train carrying the payroll arrived from Salt Lake City twice per month. To confuse would-be robbers, however, E. L. Carpenter, the paymaster for the Pleasant Valley Coal Company, never paid the workers on the same day. Instead, payday was announced by a certain blast of the mine whistle, at which time the workers would gather around PVCC headquarters to receive their wages.

When Cassidy and Lay were not watching the trains and train schedules, they were selecting locations at which to place getaway horses along the escape route. They decided it should be easy enough to take the payroll and, with the help of the relay mounts, outdistance the posse to Robber's Roost, almost one hundred miles away. While they were making their plans to rob the payroll, Cassidy used the opportunity to get his horse accustomed to the sudden blasts of the train whistle. Because the site selected for the robbery was close to the train depot, Cassidy feared his normally skittish mount would be frightened by the noise. To prepare his getaway horse, he would regularly ride him next to locomotives as they arrived in town and approached the station.

It took Cassidy and Lay about one week to learn what they needed to know. Just before noon on Wednesday, April 21, 1897, the train carrying passengers, goods, and the company payroll was heard in the distance approaching the town. Moments later, the Denver and Rio Grande Number 2 pulled up to the loading platform next to the depot. As the passengers were stepping out of the cars, the mine whistle blew, announcing payday. Within minutes, miners and others began to gather in town in anticipation of their bimonthly pay.

Cassidy and Lay mingled with the growing throng of workers and tried to look as inconspicuous as possible. Lay was on horseback, holding the reins to Cassidy's mount. Cassidy was seated, slouched on a wooden crate near the wooden stairway that led to the second-floor offices of the Pleasant Valley Coal Company in one of the town's largest buildings. As Cassidy learned earlier, the payroll was to be delivered to this office.

With the sound of the locomotive chuffing at the depot, paymaster Carpenter, accompanied by his deputy clerk, T. W. Lewis, came out of the second-floor office, descended the stairs, and hurried over to the depot. Some reports claim he was accompanied by two clerks. After crossing the tracks and entering the station, Carpenter was greeted by the express car messenger who handed over to him a leather satchel containing currency and checks. He also passed to the paymaster three canvas sacks: one of the sacks contained gold coins, and the other two were filled with silver. The total value of the payroll, according to records, was $9,860. Carpenter carried the satchel and one sack of coins, and Lewis hoisted the remaining bags. Toting their burdens, the two men left the station, crossed back over the tracks, and headed back toward the wooden steps leading to the PVCC payroll office.

When Carpenter and Lewis were still several paces from the stairway, Butch Cassidy casually rose from his seated position and confronted them. He pulled his revolver, placed the point of the barrel within an inch of Carpenter's face, and commanded the two men to release their parcels, raise their hands, and step away. The frightened Carpenter dropped the satchel and sack he was carrying immediately, but assistant Lewis turned and bolted toward the front door of the building, still holding onto one of the sacks of silver.

By this time, Lay had ridden up, leading the spare horse. Cassidy picked up the satchel and the two sacks of coins. He tossed the sacks to Lay, who was forced to drop the reins to Cassidy's horse to catch them. The mount, already high strung and sensing the nervous excitement, broke away and ran down the street. Holding tightly to the two bags of silver, Lay spurred his horse in pursuit of the other, catching him about a block away. Clutching the satchel, Cassidy waved his revolver at the gathering crowd, telling them to stay where they were so no one would get hurt. He then turned and ran to meet Lay, who was leading the second horse back up the street.

Cassidy leaped into the saddle, and together the two robbers raced down the street toward the town limits as dozens of onlookers stared in shocked silence. Before the two bandits were out of sight, shots were fired at them from the second-floor office of the coal company, presumably by the deputy clerk.

Cassidy and Lay had almost reached the town limits without experiencing any harm or resistance. Because it took such a long time for a posse to become organized, the two outlaws had time to stop, dismount, cut the telephone wires, remount, and continue their escape. (Some have claimed Meeks and Walker may have been stationed some distance out of town to cut the telegraph wires.) During the stop, the currency was removed from the satchel, which was discarded. The outlaws also apparently decided to abandon one of the sacks of coins because it was too difficult to transport, leaving behind $860 in silver.

A town resident named Frank Caffey climbed into his buggy and undertook a half-hearted pursuit of the robbers. Near the town limits, he found the abandoned payroll satchel. Nearby lay the bag containing the silver.

As Cassidy and Lay rode away to the south toward the town of Helper, paymaster Carpenter hurried to the depot to telegraph the sheriff at Price and quickly discovered the lines were dead. Noticing the locomotive was still running, he jumped into the cab and ordered the engineer to uncouple the engine from the rest of the train and make haste to Price where he would alert the sheriff in person.

It has been written that, as the locomotive passed out of the town limits gathering speed, Carpenter and the engineer both failed to notice Cassidy and Lay hiding behind a section house located near the tracks. The likelihood, however, is that the outlaws were trying to get as much distance between themselves and Castle Gate as possible.

Eventually, posses from Price, Huntington, Castle Dale, and Cleveland were formed and attempted to either overtake or intercept the bandits. Along their escape route, the outlaws bypassed the major roads, preferring to cut across unsettled country. Occasionally when they encountered a telegraph line, they cut it, further frustrating the coordination of pursuit. The posses, apparently inept to begin with, remained confused and ineffective. In one instance, a posse was so convinced another posse was the gang of outlaws they were pursuing that they opened fire on them, wounding at least one.

Following the holdup, Cassidy, after separating from his companions, rode to the Dan Hillman Ranch, located along the east flank of the Big Horn Mountains. He posed as a traveler, introduced himself as LeRoy Parker, and was offered a meal. Following dinner, Cassidy asked rancher Hillman for a job and was hired to mend fences, milk cows, and put up hay.

Hillman was quickly impressed with this new hand who worked harder than any of his others. Parker, as the stranger called himself, quickly established a friendship with Hillman's thirteen-year-old son, Fred. During his stay at the Hillman Ranch, Parker also taught the youngster how to shoot.

One afternoon while loading hay from the field onto the back of a wagon driven by Fred, Parker spied a rattlesnake. Impaling it with the tines of his pitchfork, he tossed it onto the wagon, much to the terror of the young Hillman, who leaped from his perch onto the ground. All enjoyed a good laugh over the incident, and young Fred Hillman never forgot the man who befriended him during his brief stay at the Hillman Ranch.

Occasionally, Parker was visited by a friend, and the two men were often seen engaged in quiet conversation. Years later, Fred Hillman recalled that Parker called his friend "Elzy."

One morning, Parker failed to appear for breakfast, and Fred was told to go to the bunkhouse and summon him. On arriving at the bunkhouse, Fred found a note stuck in the door that read, "Sorry to be leaving you. The authorities are getting on to us. Best home I've ever had. LeRoy Parker (Butch Cassidy)."

Cassidy and Lay eventually arrived at Robber's Roost, carrying with them approximately $7,000 in gold and silver coins and a large wad of currency without encountering any lawmen. According to a number of sources, none of them verifiable, Cassidy and Lay cached some of the gold at some secret location in the Wind River Mountains.

On June 28, 1897, the Belle Fourche, South Dakota, bank was robbed. To this day, there remains controversy over who participated in the holdup. Some have tried to link Cassidy and Elzy Lay with the robbery, pointing out that both were in the area at the same time. No evidence, however, has ever surfaced to suggest such was the case. Some are also certain that Harry Longabaugh was one of the bandits, but the contention lacks substantiation. The consensus is that the robbery was committed by at least four, perhaps as many as six, bandits, with one of them most likely being George "Flatnose" Currie. Three others, according to a wanted poster that was issued within days of the robbery, were Harvey Ray and two men both given the last name of Roberts.

The identity of the man called Harvey Ray has never been established, the name probably being an alias. The two Roberts may very well have been Harvey Logan and his younger brother, Lonnie.

During May 1898, it was reported that Butch Cassidy and Joe Walker had been shot and killed by lawmen following another robbery. The bodies of the two dead men were transported by wagon to the town of Price where they were "positively" identified by authorities as Cassidy and Walker.

According to Betenson, Butch Cassidy, on learning he had been killed by lawmen, traveled to Price and, hiding in a covered wagon, viewed the body of the dead man through a hole in the canvas. If true, the event was yet another manifestation of Cassidy's keen sense of humor. Later, Cassidy allegedly told relatives he thought "it would be a good idea to attend his own funeral just once during his lifetime."

While Cassidy observed the remains of the misidentified dead man, he was taken aback by the behavior of the crowd of onlookers. A large number of mourners passed by, many of them women who were crying.

The dead man who was identified as Cassidy was placed in a coffin and buried the following day. As a result of some concern expressed by several law enforcement authorities, the body was exhumed a short time later and the dead man subjected to another identification. Cassidy's lawyer, Douglas A. Preston, along with Uinta County sheriff John Ward, was summoned to make an identity. It has been written that Preston was so relieved the body was not that of his friend Cassidy that he undertook a celebration and stayed drunk for almost a week. The dead man was subsequently identified as John Herring, a petty outlaw known to rob travelers.

Much to the dismay of lawmen, Butch Cassidy was still alive.

SEVEN

Enter the Sundance Kid

The Sundance Kid, whose real name was Harry Alonzo Longabaugh, has been inextricably linked to Butch Cassidy, most likely as a result of the popular 1969 Western movie *Butch Cassidy and the Sundance Kid*. In the film, as well as in subsequent print and film treatments, the two outlaws appear as boon companions, participating in bank, train, and payroll robberies together throughout their bandit careers, in both the United States and South America. At least, so goes a major Western mythology that has been created in recent years.

In truth, Cassidy and Longabaugh were involved in a number of holdups, and, along with the woman known as Etta Place, traveled to South America where they participated in a series of adventures. The development of the close friendship and bond between Butch Cassidy and the Sundance Kid was created for the film, but it nevertheless forged public perception as it related to the two outlaws, even though it was overstated and often exaggerated.

For the better part of Cassidy's outlaw career in the United States, the Sundance Kid was a relative latecomer. Most of the time, Cassidy's more or less constant companion and best friend was Elzy Lay.

Butch Cassidy researchers are unsure about when he met Longabaugh, and there are a number of possibilities to choose from. Most agree, however, that the two became well acquainted in Brown's Park a short time after Butch returned from prison.

Longabaugh was born near Phoenixville, Pennsylvania, in the year 1867, the last of five children of Josiah Longabaugh and Annie Place. Phoenixville is located just a few miles northwest of Philadelphia. The elder Longabaugh was the son of German immigrant Conrad Langenbach who came to the United States as an indentured servant. (Surnames were often changed on purpose by immigrants or accidentally by immigration officials.) According to writer Donna B. Ernst, Langenbach served in the Revolutionary War.

Josiah Longabaugh was a common laborer who found it necessary to relocate often in order to find work. For the most part, the family was poor. Much of Harry's youth was spent leaving one location and settling in another, and remaining in none of them long enough to consider them home or make many friends. One of the few constants in the lives of the Longabaughs was church—Josiah and Annie were devout Baptists and encouraged their children to participate in worship services regularly. Besides Harry, who was the oldest child, the Longabaugh's had four other children—two boys, Elwood and Harvey, and two girls, Emma and Samanna.

By all accounts, Harry Longabaugh's youth was unsettled and characterized by instability, and he often found refuge in reading books. In fact, during this time one of his proudest possessions was his library card.

When he was thirteen years old, young Harry went to live with the Wilmer Ralston family in West Vincent, Pennsylvania, about ten miles from Phoenixville. Though technically in the employ of the Ralstons, Harry was little more than a servant. After Samanna married in 1880, Harry sometimes lived with her and her husband, Oliver Hallman, a blacksmith. Harry was never close to his family, save for Samanna.

According to research, when Harry was fourteen, with only a few years of education, he left home and began wandering from one sorry job to another.

During this time, it is believed that Harry Longabaugh discovered dime novels and used any and every spare coin he could save to purchase the books. He quickly became engrossed in the subject of the Civil War and in the adventures and escapades of outlaws and desperadoes of America's Wild West.

It has been written that, likely as a result of the influence of the novels, Longabaugh purchased a pistol and learned to shoot. In a short time, he became quite skilled with the weapon and manifested a deadly aim.

In the process of looking for work, Longabaugh traveled to Philadelphia, New York, and Boston. Here and there he managed to hold down a menial job for a time but had no success in securing work that held his attention for long or that paid him a living wage. In 1882, when he was fifteen years old, Harry moved to Illinois to live with his cousins,

George and Mary Longenbaugh. (Different clans of the Longabaugh family spelled the surname different ways.) On the Longenbaugh farm, many believe, Harry began learning the horsemanship skills for which he was later known.

George and Mary Longenbaugh perceived greater opportunities for making a living in the West, so they sold their Illinois farm, packed up, and moved to Colorado. After settling near Durango, George raised horses and hired Harry to break and train them. After two years, George and Mary decided life would be better for them in Cortez, forty miles to the west, so they moved again. Around this time, Cortez was little more than a tent city.

Harry continued to work for George breaking and training horses while at the same time holding down a job at a nearby ranch. George and Mary Longenbaugh grew quite fond of cousin Harry, even naming one of their sons after him. During his early residence in Cortez, Harry grew even more proficient with his horsemanship.

During this time, a number of outlaws, including Butch Cassidy, Matt Warner, Dan Parker, and the McCarty brothers, lived in the area, and though there is no record, it is likely Longabaugh encountered them.

A short time later, it is believed, Longabaugh hired on with a cattle drive to Montana. He arrived near Miles City in 1886 and found a full-time job on the N Bar N Ranch. He was nineteen years old. During his stay in Montana, some researchers contend that Longabaugh met Butch Cassidy and Matt Warner. He also became acquainted with another member of the Wild Bunch, Harvey "Kid Curry" Logan.

Like many other cowhands, Longabaugh suffered the consequences of the disastrous winter of 1886–1887, the worst ever in the history of Wyoming. Throughout much of the American West, cattle froze to death and cowhands were laid off. Out of work and out of money, Longabaugh traveled to the VVV Ranch near Sundance, Wyoming, on the Belle Fourche River. On February 27, 1887, hungry and desperate, Longabaugh stole a horse, saddle, bridle, a pair of chaps, and a pistol from two cowhands named Alonzo Craven and Jim Widner and fled back toward Miles City.

Before he could effect a complete escape, the now twenty-year-old, out-of-work cowboy was overtaken and arrested by Crook County sheriff James Ryan on April 8. Locked in handcuffs and leg irons, Longabaugh was placed aboard a train to be returned to Sundance. Since Ryan had a previous business appointment in St. Paul, Minnesota, the prisoner was forced to accompany the sheriff on the long journey before being turned in to the authorities at Sundance. At one point during the train ride near Duluth when Sheriff Ryan went to the bathroom, Longabaugh slipped out of the shackles and leapt from the moving train. Ryan ordered the train halted immediately and led a search for the fugitive, even offering a $250 reward. It was all for naught, for the slippery Longabaugh was nowhere to be found. It has been suggested that Longabaugh was aided in his escape by a confederate and that the ally was Butch Cassidy. No evidence to verify this notion, however, has been forthcoming.

Illogically, Harry Longabaugh headed straight back to Miles City after escaping. Along the way, it is believed he stole seven horses and sold them in the small town of Benton, Montana. Longabaugh was finally located and arrested again in June, this time by Deputy Sheriff E. K. Davis and stock inspector W. Smith. Shortly thereafter, he was taken to the Sundance jail in shackles and chains. There, he was tried for horse theft, found guilty, and subsequently sentenced to serve eighteen months of hard labor.

Since Longabaugh was a young man and his crime was borne of desperation, the judge proved relatively lenient. He allowed the cowhand to serve out his sentence in the county jail rather than the overcrowded Wyoming Territorial Prison in Laramie. During his incarceration, Longabaugh, along with other prisoners, made at least two attempts to escape, each one a failure. In spite of his spotty prison record, Longabaugh was finally released on February 4, 1889, and granted a full pardon by Wyoming governor Thomas Moonlight. While in jail, as one story goes, Longabaugh had acquired the nickname by which he was known for the rest of his life and throughout history—the Sundance Kid. Others have suggested a fellow Wild Bunch member provided the nickname weeks after he was released from prison.

Now twenty-two years of age, the ex-convict was once again on his own. Blond, blue-eyed, and sporting a mustache, the tall and straight Longabaugh was often described as "handsome." He was generally well dressed and well groomed, wearing monogrammed shirts, a vest, a clean and pressed suit, and a Stetson derby.

A Pinkerton National Detective Agency file on Longabaugh referred to his hair as combed into a "pompadour, it will not lay smooth." The same file stated Longabaugh "carries his head down not showing his eyes . . . bowlegged . . . walks with feet far apart. Carries arms straight by his side, fingers closed, thumbs sticking straight out."

For a while, he had a gold tooth but eventually replaced it with one made of porcelain. Women found him attractive, and they constantly sought his attention. Longabaugh was known to frequent houses of prostitution.

Longabaugh's personality has remained somewhat elusive and often contradictory to researchers. People close to him described the outlaw as "likeable," "friendly," "loyal," and "kind-hearted." On the other hand, others have referred to him as "sullen," "morose," and "mean-tempered." It was well known that, when Longabaugh was drinking, he tended to become irritable and short. Lula Parker Betenson called the Sundance Kid a "killer," but it remains unclear how she arrived at that description.

Several who have studied Longabaugh in depth believe that, rather than sullen, he was simply very reserved, perhaps even aloof, and maybe even a bit defensive in the company of people who were not his close friends.

Still in need of work, Longabaugh traveled by stagecoach to South Dakota but had little luck in finding a job. He eventually came to the town of Deadwood, a bustling mining town filled with saloons and gambling dens. Here Longabaugh likely learned the tricks of the gambling trade.

Also in Deadwood, the Sundance Kid took up company with a number of outlaws, including the killer, Bob Minor, also known as Buck Hanby. Longabaugh was with Minor when lawmen caught up with the outlaw and shot him dead. Incensed by the act, Longabaugh threatened to kill Deputy Sheriff James Swisher in revenge for Minor's death. In turn, Swisher, presumably out of fear that Longabaugh would kill him, filed complaints against the Sundance Kid. Believing his life was in jeopardy if he remained in the area, Longabaugh returned to Cortez, Colorado, to go back to work breaking horses for his cousin George.

After working for a short time with his relatives in Colorado, Longabaugh began running with Butch Cassidy, Matt Warner, and Tom McCarty. Though no solid evidence exists, it is believed by some that Longabaugh may have been involved with the robbery of the San Miguel Valley Bank in Telluride.

Longabaugh eventually returned to Montana and worked on ranches for a time. He also ventured into Alberta, Canada, where he broke and trained horses for the H2 Ranch near Fort Macleod. It is believed he also worked for a short time for the Calgary and Edmonton Railway near High River. While employed at Alberta's Bar U Ranch, Longabaugh was described by a fellow wrangler as "thoroughly likeable, a general favorite . . . a splendid rider, and a top-notch cowhand," according to Edward M. Kirby in *The Rise and Fall of the Sundance Kid*.

By autumn 1881, Longabaugh had returned to Montana. As he was broke with no prospects of finding work, he decided to rob a train. On September 29, 1892, Longabaugh, along with two companions named Bill Madden and Harry Bass, robbed the Great Northern Number 23 train near the town of Malta. The robbery was a disaster—the take was tiny, only $19, and the three outlaws, who apparently never got far from town, were arrested two days later. Bass and Madden were apprehended while drinking heavily in a Malta saloon. The two were eventually tried and sentenced to prison. A short time after Bass and Madden were apprehended, Longabaugh was arrested at the Malta train depot but soon escaped and fled southward, finally arriving weeks later at the Hole-in-the-Wall hideout near Kaycee, Wyoming.

During the next few years, the Sundance Kid pursued his outlaw career, which mostly involved cattle rustling and horse theft. His escapades may have paralleled many of those he had earlier read about in the dime novels, and his adventures carried him to Colorado, Wyoming, Montana, and even into Canada. In 1895, he was back working for the N Bar N Ranch, which had moved from Miles City to Oswego.

Sometime during this period, Longabaugh met Etta Place, a mysterious woman of great beauty and poise. By 1897, Longabaugh and Place had arrived at Robber's Roost, where they reportedly lived in a canvas tent next to ones occupied by Butch Cassidy and Elzy Lay and their respective female consorts. Here, the Sundance Kid became part of the Wild Bunch that, at the time, included Cassidy, Lay, Harvey and Butch Logan, Ben Kilpatrick, Charley Hanks, Will Carver, and George "Flatnose" Currie.

In time, and as a result of his outlaw activities, Harry Longabaugh—the Sundance Kid—somehow gained a reputation as the fastest gun in the West. Mostly, he was known as an ill-tempered, hard-drinking man who was often difficult to get along with.

As with many outlaws, public perception of Longabaugh and the actual truth may have been far apart. In all likelihood, Longabaugh, a rather complex man, possessed equal parts daring, charm, sense of adventure, and sense of style. It is clear he did not possess much of a sense of humor as did Cassidy.

Scholars have often wondered why Cassidy and Longabaugh, being opposites in so many ways, paired off as partners. The answer is simple and not nearly as complicated as the personalities of these two men. They were both very proficient and quite accomplished at what they did for a living. They could each depend on the other to carry out his responsibilities. In the outlaw world, little else is needed.

EIGHT

Growth of an Outlaw Reputation

Prior to being sentenced to the Wyoming State Penitentiary, Butch Cassidy was regarded as little more than a small-time outlaw, a horse thief. During this time, horse thieves were common, and Cassidy's conviction did little or nothing to distinguish him from others who were engaged in this illegal practice. Furthermore, save for those living in a relatively isolated geographic area, few people at this time had ever heard of the Wild Bunch.

This was all about to change.

During the next several years, Butch Cassidy, Elzy Lay, and the rest of the gang perpetrated a number of daring railroad and bank robberies, events that were to forever solidify their reputation as outlaws. As the gang's activities increased, the mere mention of the Wild Bunch struck fear into the hearts of bankers, railroad executives, and owners of large cattle empires.

As the reputation of the Wild Bunch grew, almost every train and bank robbery in Colorado, Utah, Wyoming, and other states, as well as many, if not most, of the horse and cattle thefts that occurred, was attributed to Cassidy's gang whether they were involved or not. Their reputation grew.

Although Cassidy might have been convinced his outlaw activities were a form of retribution or personal vendetta against the authority represented by banks, railroads, and the law, he surrounded himself with dyed-in-the-wool bad men who robbed and killed for no motivation other than personal gain and meanness.

In between the holdups and rustlings perpetrated by the Wild Bunch, according to Lula Parker Betenson and others, Cassidy, Lay, and outlaw Harvey Logan occasionally lived and worked on a ranch just north of Alma, New Mexico. They were going by the aliases Jim Lowe, William McGinnis, and Tom Capehart respectively. The owner of the ranch, a man named Captain William French, who was not aware of the true identities of his new cowhands, noted that his losses due to rustling came to a halt at the time the three were hired. In fact, his herd actually increased. French further commented on the competence and impressive livestock-handling abilities of the three men, and remarked that all three were extremely well behaved and courteous. French had no reason to suspect the new hands he had employed were outlaws or were, in part, using the ranch as a hideout while they planned train robberies. Cassidy was well liked by French and was made assistant foreman shortly after being hired.

Harvey Logan, the dark-complexioned companion of Butch Cassidy, was sometimes referred to as the "Tiger of the Wild Bunch" as well as the "Assassin of the Wild Bunch." It is believed Logan was born in Iowa, raised in Missouri, and came west to eventually rise as one of the leaders of the gang. Considered to be fearless, deliberate, and a born killer by many, Logan was once reputed to have ridden two hundred miles just to kill a man who informed on him.

Meanwhile, as the three outlaws pursued their cowhand duties, they made plans to rob a train. While Cassidy promised Wyoming governor W. A. Richards that he wouldn't rob banks or rustle cattle in Wyoming, he had never said anything about trains.

Though accounts and researchers differ, most agree that Cassidy masterminded what has since been referred to as the Wilcox train robbery. Some researchers have maintained that Cassidy was not even present at the robbery, but they have never provided sufficient evidence in support of that claim. The presence of the Sundance Kid has likewise been questioned. The Pinkerton National Detective Agency believed the robbery was masterminded by Harvey Logan but likewise never provided any details to substantiate their position.

The general consensus is that Cassidy and the Wild Bunch stopped the westbound Union Pacific Overland Limited Number 1 at 2:09 a.m. on June 2, 1899, near Wilcox, Wyoming, by standing on the tracks and swinging a red lantern, a commonly used technique to alert train engineers there was an emergency ahead. Though often debated, most agree that, in addition to Cassidy, gang members present during the Wilcox robbery were George "Flatnose" Currie and Harvey Logan. Other Wild Bunchers at the scene likely included Will Carver, Ben Kilpatrick, Elzy Lay, Harry Longabaugh, and Harvey Logan's brother, Lonnie.

Once the train came to a halt, two men believed to be Cassidy and Logan, both wearing masks, commanded engineer W. R. Jones and a fireman named Dietrick at gunpoint to proceed across a bridge a short distance away. When Jones refused, Logan slashed him viciously across the face with a knife. Convinced it would be fruitless to argue with the strangers, the engineer did as he was told. A few moments after the entire train crossed the bridge, the structure, which had been charged with dynamite, exploded but failed to collapse into the ravine below.

Members of the gang then uncoupled the passenger coaches from the express and mail cars and ordered Jones to move the train another two miles up the track where he was to stop. At that point, four additional outlaws appeared and, brandishing rifles and pistols, stood guard over the train.

Cassidy and at least two other robbers approached the express car and beat on the door, ordering the messenger inside to open it. The messenger, Ernest Charles Woodcock, refused and left the door bolted. The masked men placed a charge of dynamite at the bottom of the heavy door and retreated a respectable distance. The subsequent explosion blew the large iron door several yards from the tracks and caused significant damage to the express car. Miraculously, messenger Woodcock, though injured, survived the explosion—he suffered several cuts and a possible concussion. As Woodcock was carried from the car, one of the outlaws wanted to shoot him, but Cassidy interfered, stating that the courageous messenger deserved to live.

The outlaws quickly revived the bleeding and groggy messenger and ordered him to open the safe. In spite of his weakened condition, Woodcock continued to refuse the outlaws. The bandits then attached another charge of dynamite to the safe and blew away the thick steel door. In the process, they also demolished most of the express car.

The fact that Woodcock and the engineer Jones were harmed was unusual for one of Cassidy's robberies. Cassidy was never known to have stolen money or valuables from passengers and never intentionally harmed anyone other than corporations, railroads, and large ranching enterprises. In some cases, Cassidy was known to admonish gang members who attempted to rob or endanger innocent bystanders.

When the door to the safe was exploded, the money inside was blown into the air, forcing the bandits to chase it in the direction it was carried by the wind, scooping currency out of the air and from the ground. After stuffing the bills into their saddlebags and walking to where their horses were hidden in a nearby grove of trees, the bandits mounted up and rode away, making off with just over $30,000.

The outlaws split up, with half of them going in one direction and the other half taking another. A short time following the robbery, a heavy rain fell and washed away their tracks. According to Union Pacific detective F. M. Hans, the robbers traveled over 1,500 miles during their escape, all the while being pursued by three to four hundred men. "Time and again they have been surrounded by ten times their number," wrote Hans, "yet by the display of their desperate nerve and knowledge of woodcraft have managed each time to get away" (in Richard Patterson's *Butch Cassidy: A Biography*).

After learning of the Wilcox train robbery, Union Pacific officials went into action. From Cheyenne, they dispatched a special train, which carried what amounted to a small, heavily armed private army of enforcers and trackers including several Pinkerton agents. Additionally, one of the largest posses ever formed in the United States was assembled—over one hundred men provided with sturdy horses, firearms, and even bloodhounds.

Though the train robbers scattered, one pursuing group tracked Longabaugh, Logan, and several other outlaws and caught up with them at a remote cabin near Casper Creek at Horse Ranch. The posse, led by Converse County sheriff Josiah Hazen, consisted of several other prominent lawmen including Moab sheriff John Tyler and his deputy Sam Jenkins, as well as Natrona County sheriff Oscar Heistad. During a subsequent gun battle, Hazen was shot in the stomach, presumably by Harvey Logan. Hazen died later after being transported to Douglas. During the weeks that followed, the vengeance-minded Logan turned the tables on the posse members—he allegedly hunted down and killed Tyler and Jenkins.

Eventually, the outlaws met at the Burnaugh Ranch northeast of Lander to split the train robbery loot. Though his presence at the Wilcox train robbery is often debated, Butch Cassidy is known to have been at the Burnaugh Ranch for the division of the booty. In fact, he received a significant share of it, lending credence to the belief he participated in the holdup.

Rumor persists that Cassidy buried a large portion of his share near South Pass, intending to return for it later. The location of his cache was exactly in the center of a rectangle formed by four large trees; on one of the trees, the outlaw nailed a horseshoe. A fire subsequently burned over this area, obliterating almost all of the trees, and when Cassidy returned he was never able to find any of the loot.

Today, Wilcox is only a memory. Now considered a ghost town, there is hardly any evidence it ever existed save for a small sign near the railroad tracks, located approximately fifteen miles southeast of Medicine Bow in the southeastern part of Wyoming.

When it was learned that rewards totaling $118,000 were being offered for Butch Cassidy and the members of his gang, hordes of bounty hunters and lawmen became interested and began trailing the train robbers. The rewards also attracted the Pinkerton National Detective Agency, which was hired by the Union Pacific Railroad. The Pinkertons quickly assigned operatives Charles A. Siringo and O. W. Sayles to the chase. Sayles is sometimes identified as W. O. Sayler, but it is very likely that both names were aliases. The two Pinkerton men spent considerable time and energy in fruitless attempts to corral the Wild Bunch. Siringo, originally from Texas, was a nationally renowned manhunter, mostly as a result of his own boasting and self-generated publicity. Though Siringo worked hard building a reputation for himself, the detective was in fact quite good at his profession and he experienced a number of significant successes as a detective. None of his accomplishments, however, had anything to do with his pursuit of Butch Cassidy and the Wild Bunch.

Ace tracker and noted outlaw hunter Joe LeFors also became involved, coming close to the outlaws on several occasions but never making an actual capture.

The constant and relentless pursuit from Siringo, LeFors, and other lawmen was beginning to harry and concern the outlaws. The trackers were relentless, and the outlaws were forced to live on the run for long periods of time, barely finding time to stop long enough to feed themselves and their weary mounts. It was getting hot for Butch Cassidy and the Wild Bunch.

On July 11, 1899, another Union Pacific train was stopped and robbed near Folsom, New Mexico. It remains unclear whether Butch Cassidy was involved in this holdup, but it is a certainty that Elzy Lay was one of the bandits. A posse was quickly formed and went after the outlaws. In a short time, the train robbers were overtaken and a gunfight ensued, during which Huerfano County (Colorado) sheriff Edward Farr was killed. Henry Love, a posse member, was badly wounded and died later.

One of the outlaws, a man identified as William McGinnis, was wounded twice. Despite his pain and loss of blood, he escaped and was relentlessly pursued by other posses. He was eventually captured and placed in custody on August 16, near Carlsbad, New Mexico. Eventually, Elzy Lay, still using the alias William McGinnis, was found guilty of his part in the killing of Farr and sentenced to a life term in prison. While he was serving his time, Lay was instrumental in diffusing a riot and in the process saved the lives of the warden's wife and daughter. As a result of his heroic action, he was granted a full pardon and released on January 10, 1906. While Lay was in prison, his wife, Maude Davis, divorced him. In 1909, he married Mary Calvert. Lay remained in Wyoming for a while, working on ranches and engaging in oil exploration with his new father-in-law. Oddly, and unexplainably, Lay disappeared for a time, surfacing in California where he was employed by an irrigation company. For a while he also worked as a professional gambler in Tijuana, Mexico.

Following the Folsom train robbery, Pinkerton detective Frank Murray picked up Cassidy's trail and discovered he had been working at French's ranch in New Mexico under the name Jim Lowe. Unknown to Murray, Cassidy, a.k.a. Lowe, was also tending bar in Alma. Some researchers have written that Cassidy may have owned the bar. Murray had never seen Cassidy and apparently did not consider he would actually encounter him in the tiny community of Alma. One afternoon, Murray entered the bar and began asking the bartender questions about the Wild Bunch and Butch Cassidy. Cassidy, tending bar at the time, listened patiently to the detective's questions but professed ignorance relative to the gang's whereabouts. He even provided a free drink to the man who was hunting him.

A story is told that, within a short time after Murray's arrival in Alma, a group of local outlaws learned of his presence. After stalking him for a few days, they jumped him and were only moments away from hanging him from a tree limb when Cassidy intervened, instructing the toughs to release their intended victim. Some have challenged the veracity of this tale, but if true, it serves as yet another example of the good side of the outlaw Butch Cassidy.

Following Murray's departure, Cassidy realized the Pinkertons were closing in on him. He left the area in order to elude capture.

NINE

Betrayal

The longer Butch Cassidy lived the life of an outlaw, the more he regretted his decision to leave his parents' farm. He thought about his family constantly, especially his mother, and felt remorse for what she must be going through. Cassidy was convinced his actions brought great shame upon his mother and father and siblings, and as much as he wanted to visit them, he could not bring himself to do so.

The initial excitement of riding with an outlaw gang was fading following the deaths of several of his companions and the imprisonment of his good friend, Elzy Lay. Day after day on horseback with little sleep and unable to build a campfire to prepare a warm meal and coffee took its toll. Although Cassidy found some level of satisfaction in bringing hardship via the robberies to railroads, banks, and large landowners, he had not accumulated much money in the process. He often led a near-poverty existence, occasionally taking jobs at area ranches. The only satisfaction he derived in his escapades of the previous few years was that he had not killed or harmed anyone.

Cassidy thought long, hard, and often about reforming and going straight, about finding a job wrangling horses and settling down and raising a family. He was thirty-three and had little to show for his time on earth.

In what might seem like a surprising decision to some, Cassidy, anxious to put his outlaw past behind him, arranged for a clandestine meeting with Fremont County sheriff Charley Stough (some researchers say it was Uinta County sheriff John Ward) at a remote and seldom-used train station located near Soldier's Summit, a high pass in the mountains. The sheriff arrived by train, was dropped off, and hiked to the prescribed rendezvous about one mile from the station. Just after sundown, Cassidy arrived to find his old friend Stough waiting for him. The two, who had known and respected one another for a long time, were now adversaries where the law was concerned. After shaking hands, they sat down and discussed a number of topics. Most importantly, Cassidy asked Stough to intercede for the Wild Bunch with Wyoming governor W. A. Richards. He explained that many of the gang members, expert horsemen all, wanted to join the Rough Riders and travel to Cuba to fight for the United States. The Wild Bunch, said Butch, would be eager to offer their services for the defense of their country if they could receive amnesty for the previous offenses.

It is unclear exactly what measures Stough (or Ward) took in attempting to accomplish this aim, but amnesty was not forthcoming. Disappointed and angry, the Wild Bunch returned to their outlaw ways. In spite of Governor Richards's refusal to consider the outlaws' request, Cassidy still maintained hope that someday he would be allowed to go straight.

Consumed by his desire to change his life, and keenly feeling the increasing pressure of pursuing lawmen, in 1900 Cassidy sought and received an appointment with another old friend and Matt Warner's former lawyer, Orlando W. Powers. Powers was now a judge in Salt Lake City. When he arrived for his meeting with Powers, Cassidy was thirty-four years old, and his blond hair was streaked with grey. The lines on his face suggested hard living and stress. He was dressed in overalls and a denim jacket, and held a well-used hat in his calloused hands. After exchanging small talk for a while, Cassidy told Powers he was growing weary of running and hiding, that he wanted to put his outlaw life behind him and seek gainful employment. He inquired about the possibility of standing trial for his crimes and receiving an acquittal. Powers told Cassidy there was very little chance for such a thing because there were too many presidents and other officials of banks and railroads who wanted to see him behind bars; they would likely bring intense political pressure to see that done.

Cassidy then asked the judge point blank if there was any way he could be pardoned for his crimes and not go to prison. Powers informed Cassidy that he could be pardoned only if he was convicted. At that point, Cassidy had not been convicted of anything in Utah. He was currently wanted for questioning about his role in the Castle Gate holdup, but according to the judge, sufficient evidence leading to a conviction was lacking. Besides, Powers told Cassidy, even if he were pardoned in Utah, he could still be extradited to other states where he was wanted for crimes.

Convinced Cassidy wanted to go straight, Powers told the outlaw he would give his plea some consideration. He also informed Cassidy that he would meet with Utah governor Heber M. Wells and make a request for amnesty. At the same time, Cassidy went to visit another friend, Juab County sheriff Parley P. Christensen, who agreed to arrange a meeting between the outlaw and Wells. During the subsequent meeting, Wells suggested amnesty was a possibility unless murder was involved—under law, a murderer could not be granted amnesty. Cassidy assured him he had never killed anyone, so the governor promised to look into the matter while Cassidy remained in Salt Lake City.

During a second meeting approximately one week later, Governor Wells told Cassidy he was informed by his attorney general that he was wanted for murder in Wyoming and, because of that warrant, he would be unable to provide amnesty. Furthermore, continued Wells, while he might have some influence in Utah, his rulings would carry absolutely no weight whatsoever in other states where the outlaw was wanted, which included Colorado, Idaho, and Wyoming.

Cassidy was clearly disappointed, but Powers soon invited him to a second meeting to consider other arrangements. Powers suggested he would personally approach the railroad officials and try to get them to drop all charges if Cassidy would agree never to rob any more trains. The judge stunned Cassidy by asking him how he felt about negotiating for an honest job as a railroad guard working for the Union Pacific. Cassidy agreed to the conditions, and Powers said he would arrange a meeting at the earliest possible date.

A few days later, Powers met with Union Pacific officials who expressed surprise, relief, and enthusiasm at the offer. They not only agreed not to prosecute Cassidy if the outlaw would promise never to rob another train but also agreed with Powers's proposition to offer him a job as an express guard.

Powers explained to Cassidy that the railroads would much rather have a former outlaw on their payroll than have Cassidy stealing from them. Furthermore, once other would-be train robbers learned Cassidy was guarding a train, they would not be as likely to rob it. Powers told Cassidy that the railroad officials were interested in discussing the situation with him.

Through Judge Powers, arrangements were made for Cassidy to meet with representatives of the railroads during late 1899 or early 1900 at Lost Soldier's Pass, a stagecoach station near the foothills of Green Mountain, a hard day's ride north of Rawlins. Cassidy arrived at the selected location early and waited for the representatives of the railroad to show up. At his request, they would be accompanied by his friend and attorney Douglas A. Preston.

For the better part of a day Cassidy waited for the railroad officials to arrive, but they never did. Disappointed and angry, Cassidy penciled a note that said,

> Damn you Preston you have double crossed me. I waited all day but you did not show up. Tell the U.P. to go to hell and you can go with them.

Cassidy placed the note under a small rock where it was certain to be found. Convinced he had been deceived by the railroad company, he rode away.

Unknown to Cassidy, the Union Pacific men and Preston had been delayed by a storm and arrived at the appointed site one day late. They found the note.

Preston tried to find Cassidy to straighten out the misunderstanding but was never able to locate the outlaw. He summoned Cassidy's friend Matt Warner and asked him to try to find his companion, explain the circumstances, and perhaps convince him to agree to another meeting with the railroad officials.

Though he tried, Warner was unsuccessful in locating Cassidy. In the meantime, railroad officials were convinced Cassidy was somehow involved in the deaths of the two Utah sheriffs killed by Harvey Logan and withdrew their offer to excuse and employ the outlaw. Furthermore, they said, another train had been held up, and the robbery had all the earmarks of a job conducted by Butch Cassidy and the Wild Bunch.

It is believed by some that Cassidy held up the Union Pacific train near Tipton, located between Rawlins and Rock Springs in southern Wyoming, because he was angered at being stood up by the railroad representatives.

Had Warner located Butch Cassidy and helped arrange another meeting with railroad officials, history would most certainly have taken a different turn, and the life and times of this famous outlaw would undoubtedly be quite different from what it is today.

As with many Butch Cassidy and Wild Bunch episodes, researchers disagree as to what transpired on the evening of August 29, 1900, during what has been called the Tipton train robbery, and exactly which gang members were involved. There is some consensus that it consisted of Cassidy, Ben Kilpatrick, Harvey Logan, Harry Longabaugh, William Cruzan, and perhaps a woman, Laura Bullion, Logan's girlfriend. The modus operandi was similar to previous Wild Bunch train robberies, and it was reported the outlaws got away with approximately $55,000 and a large quantity of jewelry.

Some suggest one of the gang members, probably Harvey Logan, was aboard the train as a passenger. Others, writer John Burroughs foremost among them, suggest that at the previous stop he "darted out of the shadows beside the water tank, grasped the handrail at the rear of the tender, and swung aboard." After tying a bandanna around his face, he climbed into the engine compartment and, at gunpoint, ordered engineer Henry Wallenstine to stop the train at a prescribed location about one mile ahead. Other accounts claim the train stopped to investigate a fire on or beside the tracks, but this is highly unlikely. When the train came to a halt, conductor E. K. Kerrigan was then instructed to uncouple the mail and express cars from the passenger cars.

Much to the surprise of Cassidy and his companions, the messenger in charge of the express car was Ernest Charles Woodcock, the same one who resisted the outlaws' efforts during the Wilcox robbery over one year earlier.

After Cassidy told Woodcock to open the door before it was blown off, the stubborn, and apparently very loyal, employee once again refused. Not wanting to harm the gutsy Woodcock, Cassidy asked conductor Kerrigan to try to convince the messenger to open the door before he got hurt. Kerrigan spoke with Woodcock for several minutes, beseeching him to let the outlaws in, but he continued to refuse, stating that he would shoot the first man to enter the car.

Cassidy could not bring himself to blow out the door and subject Woodcock to harm again. He asked Kerrigan to try once more, and following several minutes of negotiation, the messenger finally slid the door open, allowing the robbers to enter. Before he allowed access, however, Woodcock took pains to hide two large packages of money, which the outlaws never found.

Cassidy attached an extremely large charge of dynamite to the big steel safe inside the car. The subsequent explosion not only blew the door of the safe open but also completely demolished the baggage car as well as the car coupled next to it.

Within an hour after stopping the Union Pacific train, Cassidy and his gang departed without harming a single person. The Union Pacific issued a news release stating that the robbers only got away with $54.

Woodcock, however, was quoted as saying the take amounted to about $55,000. It may be that the railroad company wanted real and potential thieves to believe that the trains were not carrying much money in order to discourage would-be bandits.

Following this robbery, the Union Pacific's private army, along with several posses, was once again on the trail of the outlaws. Ace tracker Joe LeFors came close to overtaking the outlaws, but the Wild Bunch, using relays of fresh horses stationed along the way, always managed to outdistance and elude him.

LeFors was considered by many to be the most competent tracker involved in the chase of the Wild Bunch. So quickly did he join the pursuit that, by late afternoon of the day following the robbery, he and members of his posse had ridden to within several hundred yards of the fleeing outlaws. Once again, the successful escape of the train robbers was due in large part to the several changes of fresh relay mounts along the escape route.

Within a few days, each member of the gang carried a $10,000 reward. On his wanted poster, Cassidy was described as five feet ten inches in height, one inch taller than when he was admitted to prison six years earlier.

Cassidy, as well as several other members of the Wild Bunch, was reputed to have buried some of the Tipton train robbery loot near their hideout at Diamond Mountain in Brown's Park.

The Tipton train robbery provided even more reason for railroad officials to do everything in their power to chase down the perpetrators and bring them to justice. In the wake of the train holdup, even more posses were now in the field searching for Butch Cassidy, Harvey Logan, and other members of the Wild Bunch.

The outlaws, particularly Cassidy, were aware that law enforcement authorities were growing closer, ever tightening their network of pursuit around them. While some of the outlaws reveled in the chase, Cassidy knew it could not go on forever—the railroads had too much money and manpower and would never give up until every member of the gang was captured or killed.

Now, more than ever, Cassidy gave thought to finding something else to do. It is also likely that, since there appeared to be no chance for amnesty or pardon, he considered leaving the United States and settling in some foreign country where nobody knew him and where he could obtain a fresh start. All he wanted to do now was get far away and begin life anew.

TEN

Winnemucca Bank Holdup

Only days after the Tipton train robbery, Butch Cassidy, Harry Longabaugh, and another outlaw named Will "Colonel" Carver arrived at a campsite on the Humboldt River some fourteen miles from Winnemucca, Nevada. Their appearance caused no concern for they were not known here, and furthermore, dozens of other cowhands were arriving in the area from surrounding locations in hope of finding work on the annual roundup on the nearby CS Ranch.

Carver was from Texas. Prior to being associated with the Wild Bunch, he had ridden with "Black Jack" Ketchum and is believed to have participated in several robberies. Carver tended to be quiet and unassuming, preferring solitude to company, and was content to take orders and follow.

While camping near the river with his companions, Cassidy made friends with ten-year-old Vic Button, son of the CS Ranch foreman. From young Button, Cassidy learned about a potential escape route through Lost Soldier's Pass and into Clover Valley. Button also unknowingly provided the outlaw with important information about the nearby town of Winnemucca.

Vic Button was fascinated by the white horse ridden by Cassidy, and Butch often allowed the youngster to feed and water it. From time to time, Button would bring CS horses out to the campsite to race Cassidy's white, but none of them could beat the animal. Cassidy grew quite fond of young Button and told him that someday he would give him the white horse.

Instead of applying for jobs at the CS Ranch, Cassidy, Longabaugh, and Carver, dressed as ordinary working cowhands, rode into Winnemucca nearly every day for ten days to observe the comings and goings at the bank. They even learned the names of the bank's employees and the hours of operation. The three men, using information obtained from Button, also scouted the lay of the land and several routes into and out of the town. The outlaws were friendly to everyone they encountered but tried to remain inconspicuous. While most published accounts claim only three men were involved in the Winnemucca bank holdup, at least one eyewitness stated there were four. The fourth bandit, if he existed at all, is completely unknown to researchers.

On Wednesday, September 19, 1900, Cassidy, Longabaugh, and Will Carver took a roundabout route into town, in some cases cutting across pastures and severing barbed-wire fences. On the outskirts of Winnemucca, Butch Cassidy and the Sundance Kid rode in, leaving Carver on the trail a short distance behind. Carver was to enter the bank a few minutes after his accomplices. Cassidy and Longabaugh tied their mounts in the alley behind F. C. Robbins Merchandise store, not far from the First National Bank of Winnemucca.

At approximately noon, Cassidy and Longabaugh casually walked to the bank and entered through the front door. A few minutes later as they were pretending to fill out some forms, Carver entered and tried to remain inconspicuous near a rear wall. Unfortunately, on the way to the bank Carver was sprayed by a skunk—within seconds after entering the establishment, patrons and employees, as well as Cassidy and Longabaugh, regarded him with understandable disgust.

Presently, Carver took a seat. In his arms he carried a rolled blanket that concealed a rifle. In the event of trouble, Carver was to bring forth the rifle and cover his companions.

Suddenly, Cassidy yelled for everyone to raise their hands. Longabaugh, holding two Colt .45s, forced cashier D. V. McBride, bookkeeper Malvin Hill, a stenographer named Calhoun, and a customer named W. S. Johnson against a wall. Cassidy walked to an office in the rear of the building, kicked in the door, pointed a gun at banker George S. Nixon, and ordered him to open the vault. As he did, Cassidy, according to a later interview with Nixon, held the barrel of his pistol to the banker's head and "a murderous-looking knife" against his throat. Cassidy and Carver began stuffing bags of coins into canvas ore sacks they brought with them. While this was going on, Longabaugh emptied a cashier's drawer and stuffed another sack full of gold coins.

The robbery went off without a hitch. When the outlaws gathered up all the money they could find, they forced the four bank employees and the customer out the back door and into the yard behind the building. While two of the bandits held guns on them, the third ran to the back of the Robbins store, retrieved the horses, and returned. After securing the heavy sacks to their saddles, the three men mounted up and spurred their horses out of the alley and down Third Street. They fled with a total of $32,640. As the robbers rode out of the alley, Nixon and the customer dashed into the bank and retrieved some firearms.

When the bank robbers turned onto Second Street, one of the money sacks came loose and gold coins spilled out onto the street. As Cassidy dismounted and began picking up the coins, Nixon and Johnson, now armed, ran out of the front door of the bank and began firing at him. They were quickly joined by several citizens who also shot at the fleeing bandits. Longabaugh and Carver returned fire, wounding one of the townsfolk.

The bandits rode east out of town, taking the Golconda Road that paralleled the railroad tracks. Interestingly, several of the townspeople set out in pursuit of the outlaws on foot and on bicycles. When Deputy Sheriff George Rose determined the escape route from his vantage point high atop the town windmill, he climbed down and ran to the nearby Southern Pacific Railroad station. Rose noted that the outlaws fled along a road that paralleled the railroad tracks, so when he reached the station, he ordered the engineer to fire up the locomotive and give chase to the bank robbers.

Before long, the locomotive was pulling close enough to the outlaws that Rose, leaning out of the cab, began taking aim and firing his pistol at them. Though the tracks paralleled the road, over one hundred yards separated them, a rather long distance for accurate pistol shooting.

The bandits fired back, and luckily one of them managed to shoot a hole in an engine pipe, causing steam to escape around the locomotive and obscuring the view of the bandits.

As the long-distance gun battle was taking place between the outlaws and Rose, a hastily assembled posse rode out of Winnemucca in pursuit.

Cassidy, Longabaugh, and Carver had stationed relay horses earlier at intervals along the escape route and as a result made good time against the pursuing posse. About eight miles from Winnemucca, the robbers stopped at the Sloan Ranch to change mounts. Ironically, one of the bandits switched his saddle to a horse belonging to the banker, George S. Nixon, who boarded his animal there.

While Cassidy, Longabaugh, and Carver were changing horses, Cassidy allegedly told an onlooking cowhand to give his white horse to the Button boy. Years later, Button recalled that he was presented the white horse that afternoon as he was on his way home from school. Button kept the horse for the remainder of the animal's life, and he once wrote that he didn't believe Butch Cassidy could have been all bad if he could remember keeping his promise to a kid.

By early evening of the day of the robbery, the posse, aided by a skilled Indian tracker, closed in on the robbers as they were riding toward Soldier's Pass. Beyond the pass, the three outlaws stopped at the Silve Ranch where they had left four horses several days earlier.

With fresh mounts, the outlaws began to outdistance the pursuers, riding northeastward toward the Owyhee River and Idaho. During the flight, one of the posse members, riding far ahead of his companions, closed to within several yards of the bandits, but when the outlaws turned and aimed their rifles at him he stopped and retreated. Finally, the lawmen gave up and returned to Winnemucca. Not long afterward, the outlaws crossed into Idaho.

A short time later, the Pinkerton National Detective Agency, backed by the Winnemucca bank, offered a $6,000 reward for the arrest of Butch Cassidy, Harry Longabaugh, and a third man, at the time not identified.

Later, when reward posters were issued, Will Carver was described as having a smooth face, having dark eyes, and smelling "like a pole-cat."

Though Cassidy, along with his companions, escaped once again with loot, he felt the pressure of the pursuing lawmen even more. He was resolved now more than ever to find somewhere else to live.

ELEVEN

Eastbound

Following the Winnemucca bank holdup, Butch Cassidy, Harry Longabaugh, and Will Carver agreed to split up for a while and meet sometime later in Fort Worth, Texas. Meanwhile, Cassidy and the Sundance Kid took a roundabout route to western Wyoming, where they visited friends and relaxed for a time. Carver, after burying a portion of his share of the bank loot, traveled to San Angelo in West Texas to visit his sweetheart.

The West was now alive with lawmen, bounty hunters, and private detectives, all looking for Butch Cassidy and the Wild Bunch. Since Wells Fargo and Company had been severely impacted by Wild Bunch depredations, they sent a team of investigators into the field, most notably Fred Dodge. Dodge was a dogged and tenacious detective who was determined to personally run down these outlaws for his employer. The Pinkertons, at the urging of the banks and the railroad companies, were also still very active in the hunt for the bandits.

Realizing the magnitude of the efforts of various agencies and authorities to capture or kill members of the Wild Bunch, Cassidy and Longabaugh began discussing the possibility of leaving the country soon and for good. South America was suggested as a possible destination. During this time, the countries of Argentina and Bolivia were similar to the American West in that they were opening up to settlement and ranching. Word about the opportunities awaiting enterprising Americans had filtered back to Wyoming from several who had made the journey below the equator. Additionally, as in the American West, outlaws from the United States were also traveling to the southern continent and finding the opportunities for robbery were promising.

Together, Cassidy and Longabaugh obtained and read information on various locations in South America. Presently the idea of moving there, far from pursuing lawmen, detectives, courts, and prisons, and establishing a ranch of some kind appealed to them. They began making plans.

After resting up for several weeks in Wyoming, Cassidy and Longabaugh rode south into Colorado where they purchased train tickets to Fort Worth, Texas. They arrived at this booming cattle town during the month of November 1900 and were soon joined by two other Wild Bunchers—Ben Kilpatrick and Harvey "Kid Currie" Logan. A bit later Will Carver arrived.

For the most part, the men spent their time around Fort Worth's Hell's Half Acre, the notorious red-light district near the Trinity River. During the previous few years, Fort Worth had grown to become an important cattle town and was fairly bursting with all kinds of activity ranging from banking to business dealings to bawdiness. Long a popular stop along the Chisholm Trail during the cattle drive days, Fort Worth was alive and active with cowboys, buffalo hunters, gamblers, salesmen and businessmen of all stripes, and prostitutes. The Half Acre itself included a few city blocks consisting primarily of taverns, gambling dens, pool halls, and houses of prostitution, all remaining open twenty-four hours per day.

At various times, according to research and legend, Hell's Half Acre was visited and frequented by outlaws Sam Bass, Billy the Kid, Jesse James, and Luke Short, as well as lawmen Wyatt Earp, Doc Holliday, and Bat Masterson. Unknown to many, future president Theodore Roosevelt was a frequent visitor to the Acre.

Law enforcement officials in Fort Worth openly tolerated the activities in Hell's Half Acre and visited the region only for emergencies. Law enforcement in the Acre was generally loose to nonexistent. It was said that the lawmen were afraid to enter the district; others maintain many political officials and policemen were paid handsomely by Acre interests to leave them alone.

The five Wild Bunch outlaws quartered at the Randall Apartments. Another writer, James D. Horan, claimed they stayed at a boarding house called Maddox Flats. It is possible the five men stayed at both places on separate occasions.

Cassidy, Longabaugh, Logan, Kilpatrick, and Carver spent most of their waking hours partaking of and participating in the pleasures Hell's Half Acre had to offer—gambling, drinking, and cavorting with the whores. Ironically, there was a bartender working in Hell's

Half Acre going by the name of Mike Cassidy. Bartender Cassidy was described as a sullen and rather silent man who was close mouthed about his past, which was rumored to be one filled with cattle rustling, horse theft, and perhaps even murder. Though never proven, many are convinced the bartender was the same Mike Cassidy who befriended a young Robert LeRoy Parker years earlier on the Marshall Ranch in Utah. It has also been suggested that Butch Cassidy came to Fort Worth because he knew Mike Cassidy was there and that the two had kept in touch with each other over the years.

One of the favorite hangouts for the five Wild Bunchers was Mary Porter's establishment. Porter was one of several Fort Worth madams whose house of prostitution catered to men of means, and following the Winnemucca bank holdup, Cassidy and his gang were certainly well heeled.

On November 21, the five friends purchased new clothes—suits, shirts, vests, boots, and derby hats. After making their purchases, they walked together along Main Street, encountering John Schwartz's photography studio on the way. Deciding to have a photograph made, the five entered the studio and posed for a picture in their new clothes. Cassidy sent a copy of this picture, along with several others, to Vic Button, the youngster he befriended prior to the Winnemucca holdup and to whom he gave his white horse. Though it has never been verified, numerous writers have claimed that Cassidy also sent a copy of the picture to banker George Nixon at the First National Bank of Winnemucca. Given what historians know of Cassidy's sense of humor and penchant for mischievousness, such an occurrence is not unlikely. For years, one such photograph hung in the Winnemucca bank, believed to be an enlargement of the one sent to Button.

In addition to the five outlaws, photographer John Schwartz also liked the picture. He liked it so much, in fact, that he made another copy and displayed it in the front window of his studio.

As it happened, Wells Fargo detective Fred Dodge was in Fort Worth acting on a tip that Will Carver might be in the area. Carver had been a member of the Black Jack Ketchum Gang that held up a train near Folsom, New Mexico, and killed a pursuing sheriff. Carver was identified by others present at the scene. Wells Fargo went into action, immediately distributing wanted posters throughout New Mexico, Colorado, and Texas. They also assigned Dodge to track down the killer.

A few days following the arrival of the Wild Bunch in Fort Worth, Dodge was passing by Schwartz's studio when he spotted the photograph. Peering closer, the detective immediately recognized Carver. Though most credit Dodge for the find, at least one researcher believes it was a Pinkerton detective who found the photograph.

After obtaining copies of the photograph from Schwartz, Dodge mailed one to the Pinkerton National Detective Agency, where operatives identified the other four men in the picture. Using the images in the photograph, the Pinkertons printed wanted posters that were subsequently distributed throughout the entire nation.

Most researchers agree that Dodge was assigned to Fort Worth by Wells Fargo as the result of information they received from an anonymous source. Though never proven, many believe the tip came from Carver's new girlfriend, a prostitute named Callie May Hunt, also known as Lillie Davis. Soon after Dodge identified Carver in the photographs, more Wells Fargo associates, as well as Pinkerton detectives, began arriving at Fort Worth, all hoping capture of the infamous Wild Bunch was imminent.

But they were too late.

By early December, after two months in Fort Worth, the Wild Bunch had scattered. During a subsequent prison interview, Harvey Logan stated that the outlaws had spotted a Pinkerton detective walking the streets of Hell's Half Acre near the apartment. Within thirty minutes, the Wild Bunch was gone.

Will Carver abandoned his girlfriend in West Texas, allegedly married Hunt, a.k.a. Davis, and returned to Wyoming. On April 2, 1901, Carver died from gunshot wounds suffered during the planning of a bank robbery in Sonora, Texas. After being mortally wounded by Sheriff Elijah S. Bryant, Carver's last words were reputed to be "Die game, boys."

Following a train robbery, Ben Kilpatrick and Laura Bullion tried to spend some of the purloined bank notes at a St. Louis jewelry store. The two were arrested. Kilpatrick was sentenced to a fifteen-year prison term at the maximum security federal penitentiary in Atlanta, Georgia. Bullion was given a five-year term.

About one year following Kilpatrick's release in 1911, he and a companion attempted to rob a Southern Pacific train at Dryden, Texas. Kilpatrick and an accomplice who was never positively identified slipped onto the train and climbed across the coal tender and into the engine where they pointed revolvers at the engineer, E. Grosh, and his fireman. They ordered the train halted. With Grosh in tow, the two bandits climbed out of the engine and walked to the express car where they told the engineer to instruct the messenger David Trousdale to open the door. As the engineer was escorted back to the front of the train, Kilpatrick climbed into the express car and began searching through parcels. As he squatted to inspect a particular satchel, Trousdale grabbed a heavy mallet and smashed it into Kilpatrick's head, crushing his skull and killing him instantly. The messenger then secured a rifle, took cover among the baggage, and awaited the return of the second outlaw. When Kilpatrick's accomplice finally arrived, he peered into the car only to be shot dead by Trousdale.

Despite the recognition given Butch Cassidy as a notorious outlaw, the somewhat less known Harvey "Kid Curry" Logan was probably the West's most famous train robber. The ultimate fate of Harvey Logan remains controversial. Many claim he was killed in a shootout with lawmen near Parachute, Colorado, following a train robbery. There is some evidence he took his own life rather than be captured. Though the dead man was formally identified at the scene as Logan, there is abundant evidence strongly suggesting the body belonged to someone else. Other lawmen who knew Logan examined the body and expressed doubt that it was the notorious Kid Curry. Amid the conflicting opinions, the Pinkertons sent one of their agents, Lowell Spence, to oversee the exhumation of the body and provide a definitive identification once and for all. It remains unclear what Spence's credentials were for establishing the identity of the corpse, but in his report he stated it was definitely Logan. A Union Pacific official who accompanied Spence, however, insisted it was not Logan. In the end, the Pinkerton National Detective Agency accepted the determination that the body did indeed belong to Harvey Logan. Years later, however, William A. Pinkerton himself expressed doubt it was Logan who was killed and was reasonably certain that the outlaw escaped and fled to South America, where he continued to pursue his outlaw career.

After leaving Fort Worth, Butch Cassidy and the Sundance Kid traveled south to San Antonio where they frequented another noted bordello, this one owned and operated by Fannie Porter, a well-known and highly successful madam. Fannie Porter's San Antonio bordello was a high-class establishment that entertained some of the city's wealthiest and most influential men. Fannie, apparently not related to Fort Worth's Mary Porter, has been described by author James D.

Horan in *The Wild Bunch* as a "shrewd woman who made a small fortune hiding out train robbers, outlaws, horse thieves, and killers for a price." Porter's girls enjoyed visits from Cassidy and other Wild Bunchers. Porter's five "ladies" looked forward to being entertained by Cassidy and his fun-loving friends. Cassidy is often described as performing tricks on a bicycle for Porter's ladies, but some researchers believe Harvey Logan also demonstrated his own exceptional riding skills on the two-wheeler.

Reportedly, Fannie Porter introduced Harvey "Kid Curry" Logan to Annie Rogers, whom some claim he later married. It is believed by some that Porter originally introduced the Sundance Kid to Etta Place, though this remains somewhat controversial. Porter also introduced other members of the Wild Bunch to notable "ladies of the evening" such as Laura Bullion, Lillie Davis, and Maud Walker.

According to most writers, Annie Rogers, originally from Texas, met Harvey Logan while she was working as a prostitute and fell deeply in love with him. She eventually followed Logan when he returned to the West and apparently believed she could convince him to settle down. Rogers claimed she remained faithful to him while he was spending time in prison in Tennessee.

Laura Bullion was from Knickerbocker in West Texas, the home of "Black Jack" Ketchum. Her father, Ed Bullion, even had a bit of a reputation as a train robber. In fact, the elder Bullion was killed during a train robbery attempt in New Mexico in 1897. For a time, Bullion was Will Carver's wife, or at least lover, and occasionally went by the alias Della Rose. Some authors have called her the "Rose of the Wild Bunch." After Carver's death, Bullion became close to Ben Kilpatrick. Bullion once tried to help Ben Kilpatrick spend some stolen money, but the two were apprehended and sent to prison.

Some have advanced the notion that Lillie Davis from Palestine, Texas, married Will Carver in Fort Worth, though no record of the union has ever been located. Most simply regard Davis as Carver's common-law wife. According to the Pinkertons, Davis was later instrumental in providing important information on the operations of the Wild Bunch to the Pinkertons, including information on Cassidy's description and his aliases.

Maud Walker, whose real name was Beulah Phinburg, was reportedly married to Harvey Logan in spite of Logan's relationship with Annie Rogers. Walker's relationship with Logan lasted only a few weeks, and no proof of a marriage has ever been found.

Before leaving San Antonio, it is believed Cassidy and Longabaugh converted all of their stolen bank notes to cash. Sometime in late December 1900, they separated. Longabaugh and Etta Place traveled to New Orleans where it is believed they were married, although no marriage license has ever been located. No one is entirely certain of what Butch Cassidy did during this time, but prior to Longabaugh's departure to New Orleans, the two friends agreed to meet in New York City during the first week of February.

After spending time in New Orleans, Longabaugh and Place then traveled to Phoenixville, Pennsylvania, where they visited his brother Harvey and his sisters Emma and Samanna. He told them he and his partner Cassidy were planning to travel to South America and purchase a ranch. It is uncertain whether or not Longabaugh was aware of it, but Pinkerton agents had been staking out the homes of his relatives. Longabaugh's visit, however, went undetected.

From Phoenixville, the couple traveled to Buffalo, checking into Dr. Pierce's Invalids Hotel and Surgical Institute. Some have speculated Longabaugh was seeking medical treatment for a bullet wound in his left leg, while others have suggested he may have been in search of relief from a serious sinus infection, catarrh, or perhaps even tuberculosis. Still others advance the notion that either Longabaugh or Etta, or both, sought treatment for venereal disease. Unfortunately, no records from the hospital exist.

Following a few days at Dr. Pierce's institute, the couple traveled to Niagara Falls. By the first week of February, they had arrived in New York City and checked into a boarding house using the names Mr. and Mrs. Harry A. Place. Place, it will be recalled, was the maiden name of Longabaugh's mother. Here, they found Butch Cassidy waiting for them. It has been reported that Cassidy was not happy to learn that Etta Place was going to accompany them to South America but eventually grew accustomed to the idea. In New York, Cassidy was going by the name James Ryan and was introduced as Mrs. Place's brother. The two men posed as Western cattle buyers.

While staying in New York for the next three weeks, the trio availed themselves of the culture the city had to offer, often dining in fine restaurants, going to the theater, and purchasing fine jewelry and clothes. Longabaugh and Etta Place visited DeYoung's Photography Studio and sat for a portrait. Most Longabaugh scholars are convinced this was intended to be a wedding portrait of the couple. Somehow, a copy of this photograph fell into the hands of Pinkerton agents, and the images of the Sundance Kid and Etta Place were eventually attached to wanted posters.

Meanwhile, Pinkerton detectives continued their search for members of the Wild Bunch and eventually discovered Cassidy and Longabaugh were in New York. Determined to capture the outlaw, the Pinkertons doubled their efforts, and during their investigation even learned the exact address of Longabaugh's temporary residence.

On learning that the Pinkertons were closing in once again, Cassidy and Longabaugh decided it was time to move on. Using their aliases, the Sundance Kid and Etta Place booked passage on the SS *Herminius* on 20 February 1901. The pair was bound for Buenos Aires, Argentina.

Here the record grows spotty and sparse. Several researchers are convinced Cassidy traveled to Argentina with Longabaugh and Etta Place. A few suggest he returned to the West to visit with and say goodbye to friends before making the journey to Argentina. A great many researchers are convinced Cassidy returned to the American West because he wanted to rob one more train, perhaps to acquire funding for the voyage and to purchase a ranch. Or maybe the outlaw merely desired to rob the train as a parting gesture directed to his long-time nemesis, the railroads.

Like many robberies perpetrated by the Wild Bunch, there is little agreement on which members of the gang participated in what has come to be called the Wagner train robbery. While controversial, most historians appear to agree that the gang included Cassidy, Harvey Logan, and Ben Kilpatrick. Other members were involved, but it is unclear who they were. The names most commonly mentioned are O. C. Hanks, Will Carver, and perhaps even a woman, Laura Bullion. A man named Jim Thornhill has also been mentioned. Some accounts list the Sundance Kid as one of the participants, but prevailing evidence suggests he was well on his way to Argentina at the time of the holdup.

The target was the Great Northern Express Number 3, called the Coast Flyer, and the plan was to attack the westbound train at Exeter Switch, some two to three miles east of Wagner, in northern Montana, not far from the Canadian border. While historians like to believe that Cassidy masterminded this robbery, it is more likely that Harvey Logan directed the operation alone, or perhaps in collaboration with Cassidy. Many lean toward Logan as the brains behind this holdup since he was quite familiar with the geography of the region and the schedules of the railroad. Wagner was located in a remote section of

Montana near the Canadian border and far from major law enforcement agencies, so the likelihood of being pursued by a large posse was not great.

Reminiscent of the Tipton holdup, one of the gang members positioned himself on board the train. Some accounts claim Harvey Logan purchased a passenger ticket on the Coast Flyer, probably at Malta, on the afternoon of July 3, 1901. Others say it was more likely Ben Kilpatrick. When it was time, Logan, or Kilpatrick, left the passenger car, climbed across the coal tender, entered the engine compartment, pointed two revolvers at the engineer Tom Jones and his coworker Mike O'Neill, and ordered them to pull to a stop at a prearranged location.

When the train was halted, gang members ordered employees to uncouple the express car from the passenger cars and then instructed Jones to pull the train some distance ahead.

Entering the express car was not difficult, but once inside the robbers were faced with another locked safe. Using dynamite, they attempted to blow it open. When the first charge was unsuccessful, they tried another. Finally, after four attempts, the safe was opened and the contents, some $40,000, was scooped up and stuffed into canvas ore bags.

Nervous gang members, stationed outside the express car, were fired upon by a Montana sheriff who happened to be a passenger on the train. Wielding a pistol, the sheriff climbed out of a passenger car and began shooting at the outlaws. Immediate return fire from several rifles forced him back into the car, and he was not heard from again. One of the nervous outlaws, seeing someone lean out of a passenger car window, raised his rifle and fired, wounding a curious eighteen-year-old girl in the shoulder. If Cassidy were indeed present at this holdup, the shooter would likely have been rebuked for his action.

After all the money had been gathered, the robbers ran to where their horses were tied not far away, mounted up, and, firing their pistols into the air, rode away.

After considerable delay, several posses went in pursuit of the train robbers but never had any chance of catching them. If Butch Cassidy had been a member of this group of robbers, as most believe he was, he must have been anticipating his trip to South America where he would join his friends and buy some land.

The Wagner robbery is believed to be the last train holdup ever conducted by the Wild Bunch.

TWELVE

South America

The South American experiences of Butch Cassidy, the Sundance Kid, and Etta Place are fraught with conjecture, conflicting and contradictory reports, exaggerated tales, careless and incomplete research, and error-filled reporting. It must also be considered that, during this time, other American outlaws came to South America and became involved in robbing banks, coaches, and payroll shipments in the manner of the Wild Bunch. Several such depredations attributed to Cassidy and Harry Longabaugh were likely the work of others. Since Butch Cassidy and the Sundance Kid had high profiles as a result of numerous wanted posters distributed throughout Argentina and Bolivia, the natives simply assumed, to a large extent, that it was those two particular outlaws and no others who conducted bank and payroll robberies.

Lack of accurate reporting and confusion concerning the identities of the perpetrators of most of these crimes has long been a troublesome business, often replete with error, speculation, and surmise. The combination of careless, false, and inadequate chronicling would eventually prove to be an important consideration relative to what we think we know regarding the lives, and perhaps the deaths, of Butch Cassidy and the Sundance Kid.

A great deal of the truly pertinent and substantive information relative to the South American experiences of Butch Cassidy, the Sundance Kid, and their companion, Etta Place, comes from researcher Ann Meadows, author of *Digging Up Butch and Sundance* (1996) who, with her husband, traveled throughout the region tracking down Cassidy fact and lore and sifting through numerous accounts and references. While Meadows's book sometimes reads like a travelogue, it does contain an impressive amount of information and documentation regarding the activities of Cassidy, Longabaugh, and Place in South America. Though some of the conclusions advanced by Meadows in her book are questionable, the publication is ultimately a product of diligent and patient research.

What is known for certain is that Longabaugh and Etta, still using the names Harry and Ethel Place, arrived in Buenos Aires in late March 1901 and checked into the Hotel Europa. According to one of Meadows's discoveries, Buenos Aires journalist Francisco Juárez wrote that Cassidy arrived with them instead of traveling to the western United States and participating in the Wagner train robbery, as many researchers have contended. If Juárez is correct and Cassidy made the trip to Buenos Aires, the outlaw apparently did not stay at the Hotel Europa, or anywhere else in Buenos Aires for that matter, for no references of such have been found. It is certainly possible that Longabaugh and Etta Place wanted a room to themselves, but had Cassidy arrived with them it is reasonable to assume he would have stayed at the same hotel as his traveling companions. The inability to formally account for Cassidy's presence in Buenos Aires lends some credence to the hypothesis that he was still in the United States, thus enforcing the notion that he was involved in the Wagner incident.

Pinkerton files support the theory that Cassidy remained in the United States and did not arrive in South America until March 1902. To further complicate this issue, however, Meadows claims she found a document signed in Buenos Aires by Cassidy on July 3, 1901, the time of the Wagner holdup.

Within a few days after arriving in Buenos Aires, the Sundance Kid opened a bank account in which, according to Pinkerton files, he deposited $12,000. During the subsequent months, it is believed the pair (or the trio, if Cassidy was with them) traveled throughout Argentina and Bolivia in search of suitable ranch land and a place to settle. In western Patagonia, near the lee side of the Andes Mountains, they found what they had been looking for in the Cholila Valley, Chubut Province, in Argentina.

Sometime in 1902, possibly April, Butch Cassidy, using the alias James Ryan, petitioned the Registry of the Colonial Land Department in Buenos Aires for four square leagues (approximately twenty-five thousand acres) of government land in Chubut. The Cholila Valley land was located near the foothills of the Andes Mountains, the nearest town being several miles away. The location was allegedly several hundred miles from the nearest railroad at the time.

As proof of intent to improve the land, the petition stated that 1,300 sheep, five hundred head of cattle, and some three dozen horses had been placed on it.

The two men eventually built, or arranged for the construction of, a cabin on the land they selected. The structure was of a style similar to those found in the American frontier West, made with hand-split and hand-hewn cypress logs. Double-hung, four-pane windows shipped from the United States were installed. The log cabin was somewhat unique in this region since most domiciles were constructed of native stone.

Beneath the floor of the cabin, according to Meadows, a secret room had been constructed, a room large enough for two or three people to hide from the law or cache a significant amount of loot. The cabin was simply furnished and described as always tidy, likely a result of the efforts of Etta Place. According to Meadows, the cabin is still standing today and is occupied.

In Argentina, Cassidy went by the name Santiago Ryan. He was sometimes called Santiago Max or Señor Don Max. Longabaugh continued using the identity Harry Place, but Etta was now Anna Marie Place, and Sundance occasionally used the name Frank Boyd. According to residents of nearby ranches, the North American newcomers were good neighbors and well liked. "Ryan" and "Place" proved to be excellent cowboys, proficient with lassos and skilled in livestock-handling techniques. The two strangers also apparently awed the local gauchos with their horsemanship.

"Ryan" likewise impressed the locals with his friendliness, helpfulness, and generosity. He was as friendly to the area Indians and half-breeds as he was with established ranchers and townsfolk, and was constantly purchasing gifts and candy for children.

When not working with cattle, horses, and sheep, "Ryan" and "Place" dressed elegantly and, when in public, displayed refined manners. When she appeared in public, Etta Place was always well dressed and looking elegant.

One of their neighbors was another North American, a Texan named Juan Commodore Perry. When he lived in Texas, he was simply John Perry and served as sheriff of Crockett County between 1891 and 1894. Perry claimed he moved to South America during the late

1800s to take advantage of the great opportunities that existed there for cattle ranching.

Another neighbor was a man named Daniel Gibbon, an immigrant from Wales, and he and Cassidy became close friends. Cassidy once confessed to Gibbon that he was suffering from a venereal disease he had picked up during an outing to one of the nearby towns.

John Gardiner lived on a sheep ranch near La Plata and was a frequent guest of newcomers "Ryan" and "Place." Gardiner, a Scot, had arrived in the area in 1890, taught school for a while, and eventually established the ranch on which he lived. In time, Gardiner learned the true identities of his neighbors, and he and Cassidy became close friends. The two men often shared books and magazines and engaged in lively discussions.

Gardiner fell hopelessly in love with Etta Place and, as a result, grew to despise Longabaugh, describing him as morose and sullen and little more than a mean, low cur.

By August of the following year, 1902, Cassidy and Longabaugh were busy raising livestock and appeared well on their way to making a success of their new ranching venture.

Around the time Cassidy filed the petition for the land in the Cholila Valley, Longabaugh and Etta Place returned to the United States. Cassidy may have accompanied the pair to Buenos Aires and remained with them until they booked passage on the SS *Soldier Prince*. According to most researchers, Etta was suffering from severe homesickness, while others claim she was in need of medical attention she was unable to receive in South America. It has also been written that she was suffering from "female problems," and a claim has been made that she may have had to have an abortion. A persistent rumor surfaced that neighbor Gardiner had gotten her pregnant.

Shortly after disembarking in New York City, Longabaugh and Place checked into a hospital and, following a brief stay, toured Coney Island. They also revisited Longabaugh's relatives in Phoenixville, Pennsylvania. Additionally, there exists evidence that the two may have traveled to San Francisco and visited Longabaugh's brother Elwood who was living there at the time.

On August 10, 1902, Cassidy wrote a letter to Mathilda Davis, Elzy Lay's mother-in-law, describing life in the Cholila Valley. Cassidy told her he came to South America because he was "restless" and that he "wanted to see more of the world." Regarding his ranching activities, he also wrote that he had "300 cattle, 1500 sheep . . . 28 good saddle horses, 2 men to do my work, also good 4 room house, wearhouse [*sic*], stable . . . and some chickens."

In the letter, Cassidy told Mrs. Davis he was living alone and had little to do with his neighbors, virtually all of whom spoke Spanish. Cassidy did not.

Longabaugh and Etta were in the United States when Cassidy wrote the letter. During the first week of August 1902, they returned to Buenos Aires aboard the freighter *Honorius*. After arriving, they checked into the Hotel Europa once again. During this visit, Longabaugh closed out his bank account on August 14, 1902, the amount therein being $1,105.50. It is believed the two then returned to Chubut Province during the third week of that month. To reach the Cholila Valley, it was necessary to take a steamer up the Chubut River to the point where the shallow channel inhibited further travel and then transfer to horses to complete the long journey back to the ranch.

Before and after Cassidy and Longabaugh arrived in South America, other American outlaws, perceiving greater opportunities in the southern continent than in the United States, made the trip. Once settled in countries such as Argentina, Bolivia, and Chile, they continued to perpetrate robberies of banks, trains, and payrolls. In a number of cases, their robberies were styled after those of the Wild Bunch—extensive and careful investigation of the robbery target and the stationing of relays of fresh horses and supplies along the escape route. As a result, the better known Butch Cassidy and the Sundance Kid were often given credit for the crimes. Two such outlaws were Robert Evans and William Wilson. Apparently the two were known to Cassidy and Longabaugh and might have even been friends. Evidence suggests the four lived together at the Cholila Valley ranch for a time. Evans and Wilson, it has been written, closely resembled Cassidy and Longabaugh.

Several months after Cassidy, Longabaugh, and Etta Place settled onto the Cholila ranch, the Pinkertons learned of their whereabouts. A local law enforcement agency received a circular from the Pinkerton National Detective Agency that contained photographs of Cassidy, Longabaugh, Etta Place, and Harvey "Kid Curry" Logan. The circular boasted a $10,000 reward for the capture of the outlaws, dead or alive. It was rumored that a Pinkerton detective actually arrived at the ranch but was shot and killed and buried someplace on the premises. Another version of this story has the Pinkerton representative alerting the provincial police, and together the two men rode to the ranch with the intent of arresting the outlaws. When they arrived, so the story goes, Cassidy and Longabaugh shot their horses out from under them and they fled on foot.

According to Gardiner, the local sheriff was well aware that the newcomers living out on the Cholila Valley ranch were Butch Cassidy, the Sundance Kid, and Etta Place but chose to do nothing. It has been speculated, either by Meadows or Gardiner, that the sheriff was also in love with Etta Place, but it is more probable that he simply feared a confrontation with the famous outlaws.

Longabaugh and Etta would return to the United States at least one more time in 1904. It is believed the two traveled to the World's Fair in St. Louis and spent time with friends in Fort Worth.

Sometime during late 1903 or early 1904, Pinkerton detective Frank Dimaio was in Brazil on other agency business when he learned that two Americans resembling Butch Cassidy and the Sundance Kid were ranching in Argentina and using the aliases James Ryan and Harry A. Place. On his next visit to Buenos Aires, the intrepid and curious Dimaio found the names "Mr. and Mrs. H. A. Place" among the list of crew members for the *Honorius*. Subsequent investigation and pursuit of clues led Dimaio to U.S. vice consul George Newbury, who lived not far from the Cholila Valley ranch of the bandits. Newbury told the detective that his neighbors were highly regarded in the community and that they gave no evidence of being notorious outlaws. Besides, he informed Dimaio, arresting Cassidy and Longabaugh during this time of the year would be difficult if not impossible—it was the rainy season, and the accompanying flooding would prevent law enforcement authorities from reaching Cholila Valley.

Some researchers have suggested that Newbury was protecting Cassidy, Longabaugh, and Place by attempting to discourage Dimaio. On the other hand, at the urging of the Pinkerton agent, the vice consul did agree to invite the outlaws to Buenos Aires with the ruse that they were needed to sign some deeds. Once there, he said, they could be easily arrested. As far as is known, however, Newbury never issued the invitation.

While waiting for the rainy season to abate, Dimaio provided Argentine police with wanted posters identifying Cassidy, Longabaugh, and others. Dimaio was then summoned back to Pinkerton headquarters in the United States where he briefed Robert Pinkerton on the situation. Pinkerton subsequently initiated a correspondence with Argentinian officials, warning them of the possibility of Butch Cassidy and the Sundance Kid renewing their outlaw ways in their country. In actuality, Cassidy and Longabaugh were law-abiding and contributing citizens of Argentina and remained quite peaceful until the Pinkertons started closing in.

It is believed that their neighbor Gardiner learned of the Pinkerton reward circular and informed Cassidy. It has also been suggested that their other neighbor, former lawman Juan Commodore Perry, had a role in the departure of the bandits. Unknown to the two outlaws, Perry had been contacted by the Pinkertons and asked to keep an eye on them. It has been written that Cassidy and Longabaugh learned of Perry's involvement with the authorities and decided to leave before it was too late.

In any case, sometime in late 1904, Cassidy and Longabaugh no longer believed they were safe in the region so, after selling their stock, buildings, and a number of personal possessions to Thomas Austin, a Chilean land company official, they fled from the ranch. By 1905, the holdings were abandoned.

No one is completely certain of the whereabouts of Etta Place during this time, but the notion of whether or not she remained with Cassidy and Longabaugh is controversial. It has been speculated that she returned to the United States permanently around this time, but some researchers believe she remained in South America and even participated in a number of Cassidy- and Longabaugh-led robberies.

Cassidy and Longabaugh, after packing only a few necessary belongings and leaving the Cholila ranch, fled to a location near a point where the Tigre River flowed into Lake Cholila. Here they established a rude camp and lived for approximately one year. As a result of the ubiquitous reward posters, the two outlaws were eventually recognized by a number of people, so they decided to move again. They traveled across the Andes Mountains and settled for a time in Chile.

The Pinkerton National Detective Agency relied in large part on external funding for a number of their efforts. In particular, the pursuit of Butch Cassidy and the Sundance Kid was financed by the Union Pacific Railroad (UPR) and the American Bankers Association (ABA). After being convinced the two outlaws were alive and well in South America, Robert Pinkerton contacted the UPR and ABA to request more funding in order to remain in the hunt and, hopefully, capture their quarry. Both organizations, however, refused, each believing that as long as the two bandits were out of the country they posed no threat to their operations. Without adequate funding, the Pinkertons pulled all of their agents out of the field but continued to monitor the two outlaws.

Butch Cassidy was living in South America when his mother passed away on May 1, 1905, at fifty-eight years of age. Cassidy's sister, Lula Parker Betenson, maintained Annie Gillies Parker, who deeply loved and constantly worried about her wayward son, died of a broken heart.

A few writers have claimed that Butch Cassidy returned to Utah for his mother's funeral, a claim not supported by any evidence. Betenson denied her brother had returned and stated that while living incognito in South America he was in no position to receive the information that his mother had passed away.

According to some, Cassidy and Longabaugh traveled to Rio Gallegos in extreme southern Argentina where they checked into a hotel room or small house. Details are sketchy, but two outlaws, going by the names Brady and Linden, held up the Rio Gallegos Banco de Londres y Tarapacá and, though estimates vary, made off with between $70,000 and $130,000. The release of information that the bank was robbed by two Americans led many to jump to the conclusion that the perpetrators were Cassidy and the Sundance Kid.

Several miles from town, pursuers found the robbers' horses, along with a third, which they had apparently exchanged for fresh ones. If Etta Place had accompanied the two outlaws to Rio Gallegos, and if it is indeed true that Cassidy and Longabaugh were the robbers, she may have been waiting for them out of town. Others suggest that the third rider was Harvey Logan who, it is theorized, may have joined the bandits for a time in South America. Several weeks later, the Pinkertons eventually admitted they were convinced Harvey Logan was in Argentina, probably with Butch Cassidy and the Sundance Kid.

Despite the inclusion of this incident in a number of treatments of Butch Cassidy and the Sundance Kid, there is no compelling evidence that the two were involved in the Rio Gallegos bank robbery. Different versions—all conflicting and contradictory—of the robbery and escape increase the doubt of what actually occurred there. Among other problems, the physical descriptions of the bandits turned out to be quite different from those of Cassidy and Longabaugh. Additionally, witnesses claimed the bandits were between twenty-five and thirty years old. At the time, Cassidy and Longabaugh were close to forty years of age and greying. Furthermore, at the time of the robbery, Cassidy and Longabaugh were reported to be hundreds of miles away.

Following the Rio Gallegos robbery, Cassidy and Longabaugh, and perhaps Etta Place and Harvey Logan, reportedly journeyed to Chile. There exists a good possibility that this quartet robbed the Banco de la Nación in the town of Villa Mercedes on December 19, 1905, escaping with the equivalent of $130,000. (Another date given for this robbery is March 2, 1906.) Typical of a Butch Cassidy holdup, there was no gunplay, although when one or more of the bank employees resisted, the outlaws struck them with their pistols. The pursuing posse reported the robbers consisted of three men and a woman. Consistent with a Cassidy mode of operation, tired horses were exchanged for fresh ones along the escape route.

When shown photographs of Butch Cassidy, the Sundance Kid, and Etta Place, a Villa Mercedes bartender identified them as visitors to his tavern just prior to the robbery. Additionally, the foreman of a nearby ranch stated the three had stayed there for a few days just before the bank was robbed, departing only hours before the holdup.

Butch Cassidy and the Sundance Kid eventually found jobs with the Concordia Tin Mines near Tres Cruces in the foothills of the Bolivian Andes, some seventy-five miles southeast of the capital La Paz. The year was probably 1906. Cassidy, going by the alias of Santiago Maxwell during this time, showed up at the mining headquarters, sought out manager Clement Rolla Glass, and inquired about a job. He was hired at $150 per month plus room and board. His duties were to purchase livestock and occasionally transport payroll remittances. In no time at all, Cassidy impressed Glass with his competence and honesty. Cassidy would be given a significant amount of cash before leaving on a horse- or mule-buying expedition. Each time, he returned with fine stock and turned over to Glass any monies left over. In a short time, mine officials were trusting Cassidy to deliver payrolls, sometimes totaling as much as $100,000.

Several weeks after Cassidy went to work for the Concordia Tin Mines, Longabaugh, using the alias Enrique Brown, joined him. Glass hired Longabaugh to break and train mules.

By this time, all trace of Etta Place seems to have vanished. The consensus is that she left South America and returned once again to the United States, this time for good. Evidence suggests she traveled to Denver, where she may have undergone an appendectomy. According to a statement made by Cassidy to a mine supervisor, Etta had no confidence in South American hospitals. He said he and Longabaugh drew straws to see who would accompany her to the United States; Longabaugh lost, so he went with Etta. Longabaugh returned to South America alone shortly afterward.

It soon became clear to Glass that "Maxwell" and "Brown" had known each other prior to coming to La Paz, and though he suspected that they possessed a dark past, he remained pleased with their work. Glass described Cassidy as "pleasant . . . cultured . . . charming . . . used good language and was never vulgar. Women . . . invariably liked him." Other officials at the mines described Longabaugh as "distant . . . sullen . . . difficult to strike up a friendship," as well as "taciturn" and "morose" (from Richard Patterson's *Butch Cassidy: A Biography*). The two men were hard workers and dependable. In time, however, the managers found out their true identities.

A man named Percy Seibert was reportedly employed as an engineer at the Concordia Tin Mines and eventually became good friends with Cassidy and Longabaugh. Author Larry Pointer wrote that Seibert was employed by a Bolivian supply company that did a considerable amount of business with the Concordia Tin Mines. Seibert's notes and recollections provide most of what we know, or what we think we know, about many of the South American activities and attitudes of the two outlaws.

Seibert met the two Americans when he returned to the mines following a purchasing trip to the United States. At first, Cassidy and Longabaugh tried to avoid Seibert, but they gradually warmed to him. The engineer grew to like the two men and enjoyed numerous conversations with them, learning much of their past as well as their hopes for the future. In time, Cassidy and Longabaugh told Seibert about their true identities, about their outlaw activities in the United States, and about being pursued relentlessly by the Pinkertons, the railroad companies, and detectives working for the American Bankers Association. They came to South America, they told Seibert, with the hope of becoming anonymous and pursuing a new and honest life, of becoming legitimate. Unfortunately for them, the large rewards offered for their capture kept lawmen, detectives, and bounty hunters hot on their trail, making life difficult for them and causing them to flee throughout the countryside. During one conversation between Cassidy and Seibert, the outlaw referred to Etta Place as a great housekeeper with "the heart of a whore."

In spite of the outlaw backgrounds of the two new mine company employees, Seibert came to trust them, particularly Butch Cassidy. One time, related Seibert, he and Glass were counting out payroll money from a large stack of gold coins when Cassidy walked into the room. Cassidy joked about how easy it would have been to steal the gold. Ultimately, Glass and Seibert trusted Cassidy to take a significant amount of the gold—believed to be worth well over $100,000—and exchange it for paper currency. Though it would have been very easy to disappear with the small fortune, Cassidy completed the job and returned, remaining true to his commitment never to rob from an employer.

Seibert listed a number of contributions Cassidy made during his tenure at the Concordia Tin Mines. Once, on learning that a group of American outlaws was planning to kidnap a neighboring businessman and hold him for ransom, Cassidy warned the intended victim and even arranged for a bodyguard. Another time, Cassidy foiled a plot to assassinate one of the tin mine officials.

Even though Seibert and Glass learned their two employees were still wanted by law enforcement authorities and that it would have been an easy task to turn them in and collect the reward money, they agreed to keep their identities secret.

Some writers, including Betenson, are convinced Cassidy returned to the United States with Longabaugh and Place around this time. During their travel, according to Betenson, Cassidy was spotted visiting friends in Rock Springs, Wyoming, but Seibert's recollections challenge this.

Clement Glass eventually left the Concordia Tin Mines, and Percy Seibert was placed in charge. During his tenure as manager, he and his wife grew even closer to Cassidy, less so with Longabaugh. The two outlaws were often invited to the Seibert residence for dinner. For obscure reasons, around this time Cassidy began using the alias "Jim Lowe."

Seibert grew very fond of Cassidy and believed he was better off having the outlaw working for him. During the time Cassidy was employed, no other outlaws came near the mines or threatened the payroll. In his memoirs, Seibert described Cassidy as sober, a gentleman, agreeable, pleasant, and trustworthy. On the other hand, Seibert was never able to establish any kind of close relationship with Longabaugh.

Cassidy's decent nature is manifested in another of Seibert's recollections. After leaving the employ of the Concordia Tin Mines, Cassidy arrived at a mining camp owned by two Scotsmen. He scouted the area, the trails, and the payroll schedules as he planned a holdup. Cassidy entered the mining camp and, posing as a down-and-out prospector out of money and food, asked for a job. The two Scotsmen offered to hire him as a night watchman, explaining they didn't really need one but they would give him the opportunity to make some money before traveling on. They also fed him well and told him to help himself to the whiskeys and other liquors they had in their own supply. Ultimately, Cassidy decided the two Scotsmen treated him so well that he did not have it in his heart to rob them.

According to Seibert, Cassidy once told him he thought Harvey Logan was the most fearless man he had ever met. He also stated he tried to get Logan to join him and Longabaugh in South America, but contrary to Pinkerton reports, Logan never showed up. He also told Seibert the second-bravest man he ever met was Ernest Charles Woodcock, the express car messenger who resisted Cassidy's attempts during both the Wilcox and Tipton train robberies.

In later years, Seibert was named the commissary general of the Bolivian Railway Commission and, according to writer Gail Drago, was "one of the most decorated Americans in South American history."

For a three-year period ranging from 1906 to 1908, the two outlaws worked at the Concordia Tin Mines. While they were afforded numerous opportunities to escape with large amounts of money and gold, the two outlaws never considered robbing their employers. On the other hand, most researchers believe, they committed robberies at other mines in other locations while they were employed at Concordia.

The longer Cassidy and Longabaugh worked at the Concordia Tin Mines, the more people became aware of who they really were, and Cassidy was constantly worried they would be discovered by law enforcement officials. Coupled with the fear of discovery was his concern for Longabaugh's growing drinking problem. During an evening spree in the nearby Bolivian town of Uyuni, the Sundance Kid became drunk and talked openly about robberies he and his companion had pulled in Argentina. Concerned, Cassidy paid the bill and hastened

Longabaugh out of the cantina. But it was too late, and word got back to the Concordia Tin Mines.

Sometime in October 1907, Cassidy and Longabaugh entered a police station in Santa Cruz, Bolivia, to inquire about directions. While they were there, they noticed wanted posters of themselves hanging on the wall. The attending policeman, however, did not recognize the two desperadoes, as Cassidy was sporting a beard and Longabaugh had, according to reports, gained a significant amount of weight.

In spite of the growing pressure, the two outlaws continued to plan and perpetrate robberies. In addition to a mine payroll here and there, there is some evidence they may have even robbed a Bolivian Railway train near the town of Eucalyptus, several miles southeast of La Paz, on August 19, 1908. According to reports, the bandits escaped with Bolivian money equal to $90,000.

Although Etta Place and Harvey Logan are occasionally linked to a number of robberies believed to have been masterminded by Butch Cassidy and the Sundance Kid during this time, no one knows for certain if Place and Logan were even in South America.

To compound the identity problems, the number of other North American outlaws who were operating in Bolivia and Argentina was increasing, and it is likely that several robberies committed by them were attributed to Cassidy and Longabaugh. The aforementioned Robert Evans and William Wilson were committing crimes in the area in much the same manner as Cassidy and Longabaugh and were often mistaken for the more famous duo. Evans and Williams, it was reported, were eventually overtaken by Argentine lawmen and killed.

Sometime in 1908, after Cassidy and Longabaugh left the Concordia Tin Mines, they took a job in the southern part of the province. For a while, the two men, using a variety of aliases, drove stagecoaches for a Scotsman named James Hutcheon.

During this time, it is believed Cassidy and Longabaugh learned about regular payroll shipments to the Aramayo mines near the southern Bolivian town of Tupiza. According to writer Arthur Chapman, who quoted Percy Seibert, Cassidy and Longabaugh decided to rob the payroll pack train.

The Aramayo payroll robbery generated a number of subsequent events that have remained among the most controversial and contradictory on the subject of American outlawry for over a century and have provided a momentum for the beginning of one of the greatest outlaw mysteries of all time.

THIRTEEN

The San Vicente Incident

Two men believed to be Butch Cassidy and the Sundance Kid robbed the payroll pack train of the Aramayo, Francke, and Cia silver mines located near the town of Quechisla. The robbery, which took place on November 4, 1908, occurred not far from the town of Tupiza, located several miles southeast of Quechisla. In addition to approximately $7,000 in payroll money taken, the bandits also escaped with one of the company's mules. The animal in question was reportedly branded with an *A*, the mine's official brand. This single mule would eventually become a key element relative to the identification, or misidentification, of the robbers.

Following the payroll robbery, the two bandits, initially identified as North Americans, allegedly rode into the town of Tupiza, where word of the holdup had already arrived. Soon after unpacking their gear, the strangers discovered the townspeople suspected them of taking the payroll. Hastily, they repacked and fled during the night, apparently bound for the town of Uyuni, located some ninety miles to the northwest.

Three days later, on November 7, according to most reports, two North Americans—believed by many to be the same ones who conducted the Aramayo payroll robbery, rode into the small Indian village of San Vicente. San Vicente is located approximately midway between Tupiza and Uyuni. By the time the strangers arrived, they had apparently ridden a long distance and were in search of a meal and a place to spend the night. The village of San Vicente was small, and there were few choices. The newcomers finally settled in a room at the police station, which also served as an inn.

While the two men were dining on beer and tinned sardines inside the room, a local constable happened to pass by. As he was examining the mules the strangers rode, he noticed that one bore the brand of the

Aramayo mines. The constable was also convinced the animal was the same one placed in the charge of a friend of his named Gil Gonzalez, a man who was in the employ of Carlos Peró. Peró was employed as a manager at the Aramayo mines and on the day of the robbery served as the chief courier in charge of the payroll shipment. The constable had earlier learned of the Aramayo robbery, and his instincts suggested to him that these men had something to do with it. He sent a runner to a nearby encampment of Bolivian troops advising them of his suspicions.

The generally accepted legend regarding the payroll robbery and the subsequent alleged shootout with authorities, the one that has been popularized via film, television, and novel, can be traced to the florid writings of Arthur Chapman in the April 1930 issue of *Elks Magazine*. In Chapman's version of the event, the captain of the Bolivian soldiers led his command to the police station and ordered his troops to surround the building. Then, with drawn revolver, he walked into the room of the two strangers, both of whom were allegedly drunk, and called for them to surrender. One of the strangers, whom Chapman identifies as Butch Cassidy, drew a pistol and shot the captain. Seconds later, the cavalry, now led by a sergeant, swarmed through the gate to the courtyard adjacent to the room. As the soldiers filled the courtyard, the strangers began firing from the room, killing more of the soldiers with the initial fusillade. The two Americans kept up their fire, according to Chapman, eventually killing several more soldiers and wounding many others. "Blood was settling in little pools about the courtyard," wrote Chapman. The Bolivian soldiers then took shelter behind the courtyard wall and commenced firing into the room, bullets thunking into the thick adobe walls of the building.

At one point during the gun battle, one of the strangers, whom Chapman identified as Harry Longabaugh, decided to dash into the courtyard and retrieve some rifles and ammunition apparently left there earlier. In Chapman's narrative, the Sundance Kid, firing his pistol, jumped over the bodies of the dead and wounded soldiers toward the rifles. Before he reached the arms, however, he was cut down by Bolivian bullets, hit at least seven times. The man had almost reached the rifles when he fell to the ground, seriously wounded. At this point, the other stranger rushed from the room and ran to the side of his fallen companion. With bullets striking all around him, and several thudding into his body, he hoisted the fallen man over his shoulder and ran back to the safety of the room.

Chapman continues, "Once inside, the rescuer saw that his friend was mortally wounded. Checking his pistols, he noted that he only had a few bullets left. Realizing it was hopeless to try to retrieve the guns and ammunition outside in the courtyard, the stranger sat back and pondered his fate."

Around 10:00 p.m. that evening, the Bolivian soldiers heard two shots fired from within the room, and then silence. Throughout the night, the soldiers fired sporadically through the windows and doors.

The following morning, the Bolivian troops maintained their vigil, shooting occasionally into the room. At noon, says Chapman, an officer, backed by several soldiers, rushed across the courtyard and into the room. To his surprise, the officer found the two men dead, apparently by their own hand. The man who ran into the courtyard to retrieve the rifles had a mortal wound through his head, seemingly killed by his companion. The other, according to the officer, was apparently a suicide.

On inspecting the belongings of the strangers, the soldiers found what was identified as the Aramayo mine payroll money. In addition, the soldiers also found some gold they believed was taken during the Bolivian Railway robbery.

So wrote Arthur Chapman some twenty-two years *after* the actual event. The source of most of Chapman's information was, interestingly, Cassidy's close friend, Percy Seibert.

Spurred by Chapman's article, numerous investigations into what had come to be called the "San Vicente shootout" were undertaken over the years. The resulting research has yielded several different versions of the gun battle, with most of them conflicting and contradictory.

As a result of the dogged and tenacious research efforts of Ann Meadows and her husband, Dan Buck, quite a bit more has been learned about the South American adventures of Butch Cassidy and the Sundance Kid, as well as the circumstances of the Aramayo payroll robbery and the so-called shootout in San Vicente. Though a great deal has been learned, and Meadows and Buck must be lauded for their efforts, no clear, indisputable accounting of the fate of Cassidy and Longabaugh has been forthcoming. As a result of contradictory, conflicting, careless, and erroneous reporting and testimony, there remains no obvious and explicit distinction between fact and fiction. The truth exists somewhere among the records and documents, but it is muddied and difficult to discern.

During her research, Meadows located some correspondence by a number of eyewitnesses to the so-called shootout, as well as missives from Carlos Peró, the Aramayo mines manager and the leader of the small group that was escorting the payroll that was robbed.

According to Peró, who was accompanied by his son, Mariano, and his servant, a man named Gonzalez, two North American bandits stole fifteen thousand bolivianos along with a mule. A description of the bandits accompanied Peró's information: one was described as heavy-set and pleasant, the other of medium weight. They both wore "new, dark-red, thin-wale corduroy suits with narrow, soft-brimmed hats."

Elsewhere, information was discovered that contained a description of one of the bandits as thin and of average build, the other taller and heavyset. Already, contradictory evidence was surfacing, and it would only get worse.

There exists a general consensus that, on November 7, two men arrived at the small village of San Vicente and were soon afterward identified as the potential payroll robbers. The only bases for this identification appears to be as follows: (1) at least one of the recent arrivals, and possibly both, appeared to be North Americans; and (2) they were strangers, unknown to any in town.

It was also learned by Meadows that only a police inspector, a San Vicente citizen, and two soldiers went to visit the strangers at their temporary residence—a total of four men, not a company of Bolivian troops, as had been related by Chapman and reported by others.

Furthermore, Meadows uncovered written recollections that stated no rifles and ammunition had been left in the patio by the strangers. The two men were, in fact, well armed inside their room and carried plenty of ammunition on their persons.

According to the information acquired, the four San Vicenteanos stationed themselves outside of the room. One, a soldier, approached the open doorway only to be fired upon by one of the strangers—allegedly Butch Cassidy. Once hit, the soldier fell to the ground and then struggled to his feet, turned, and fled. He died several minutes later at a nearby home. At this point, the San Vicente citizen decided to leave the scene and go home, and the two men remaining chose to stand guard over the room throughout the night.

The San Vicenteano who went home said he later heard "three screams of desperation," apparently coming from inside the room, and then silence. The next morning at six, according to some research, men entered the room and found the inhabitants dead, the "smaller stretched out on the floor dead with one bullet in the temple and another in the arm." The taller bandit, the one presumed by some to be the Sundance Kid, was, in death, hugging a large ceramic jug that was in the room. He had a bullet wound in the forehead and several more in his arms. Both men, according to one witness, still had their guns in their hands. Another witness claimed the taller bandit also had several bullet wounds in the chest. Following a search of the room and the belongings of the dead men, the Aramayo payroll was allegedly recovered, as well as a map of the area marked with an escape route.

Another witness stated the tall gringo was dressed in a brown cashmere suit, grey hat, red gaiters, and an ammunition belt, and carried a gold watch, a dagger, and a silk handkerchief. The shorter man wore a yellow cashmere suit, red gaiters, and a cartridge belt and had in his possession a silver watch and a blue silk handkerchief.

Both men were described as blond and unshaven with turned-up noses, the small one "ugly," the other good looking. In addition to the Aramayo mine payroll, their parcels contained an abundance of silk handkerchiefs. Some researchers have used the presence of the many silk handkerchiefs as evidence that one of the men was indeed Harry Longabaugh, who was believed to suffer from catarrh, an inflammation of the mucous membranes.

Percy Seibert, on learning of the deaths of the two men at San Vicente, stated without hesitation that they were, indeed, Butch Cassidy and the Sundance Kid. There is no evidence, however, that Seibert traveled to San Vicente and examined the bodies. Seibert told Chapman he was convinced Butch Cassidy shot Longabaugh in the head and then killed himself.

Later that day, the bodies of the two strangers were allegedly taken to the San Vicente Indian cemetery and buried in unmarked graves. According to Meadows's research, the two bodies were interred between a German miner who blew himself up while thawing out some dynamite on a stove and a Swedish prospector who accidentally shot himself while dismounting from a mule.

There, in that windswept and poor cemetery, according to Chapman, lay the remains of two of America's most famous outlaws, Butch Cassidy and the Sundance Kid.

When Meadows traveled to South America to try to learn the truth of the San Vicente shootout and burial, her efforts yielded a wealth of information heretofore unknown outside of the region. The information, consisting of documents, records, letters, personal recollections, and vignettes, provided new insight and material for study as it related to the South American activities of Butch Cassidy and the Sundance Kid. It can also be effectively argued that Meadows's research contributed more to the confusion and contradiction that surrounds Cassidy's alleged participation in the robbery and subsequent death in San Vicente than it did to eliminate it.

FOURTEEN

The San Vicente Incident Revisited

Much of what most people know, or think they know, about the fate of outlaw Butch Cassidy is derived from Arthur Chapman's 1930 description of the so-called San Vicente shootout. This article formed the basis of numerous subsequent treatments on Cassidy and his partner, and solidified in the minds of many the legend of Butch Cassidy and the Sundance Kid, along with their heroic yet ill fated confrontation with the Bolivian army.

A review of pertinent documents, however, suggests that something entirely different occurred, something quite contrary to the popular perception of the aforementioned South American events. Furthermore, the more one examines records of the time and region, the more one comes away impressed and dismayed with the overwhelming amount of conflicting and contradictory testimony, as well as a profusion of confusion relative to who, in truth, committed the payroll robbery, what actually happened at San Vicente, who was killed there, and who was buried in the San Vicente cemetery. With regard to each of the above, the identity of the participants has always remained in question. They are as much in question today as they were then.

It would be appropriate, therefore, to examine closely the circumstances surrounding the robbery of the Aramayo mine payroll, the incident at San Vicente, and the burial of the two victims who many believe were Butch Cassidy and the Sundance Kid.

The Robbery

According to various bits and pieces of information coming mostly from his own testimony, Carlos Peró, in the company of his son and a servant named Gil Gonzalez, was transporting the Aramayo payroll from Uyuni to Tupiza when he was held up on the road near Salo, located just north of Tupiza. Peró, one of the principals in the robbery and the official in charge at the time, was a man who, logically, would have and should have known as much or more about what transpired than anyone else, save for the robbers themselves.

Peró identified the bandits as Yankees who were hiding behind rocks a short distance off the trail. In one account, Peró refers to the bandits as "wearing masks." However, according to Richard Patterson in *Butch Cassidy: A Biography*, in a subsequent letter Peró says they were wearing bandannas. Some believe "masks" and "bandannas" are synonymous, but they are not; they are quite different. Perhaps Peró misspoke. One may grant that he was unaware of the difference, but that is not likely. In any event, with hats pulled low over their heads and the lower portions of their faces apparently well covered with bandannas (or other parts of their faces hidden by masks), all Peró likely saw of the two robbers were their eyes.

Peró also said the robbers were carrying rifles cocked and ready to fire. Yet, in another report, Peró contradicts himself by saying one was unarmed.

Peró described the bandits as pleasant and well mannered. After taking the money, according to Peró, they tied up the three Bolivians and left with the payroll money, one dark mule, and a new hemp rope. Yet another report stated the Bolivians were not bound at all.

The bandits departed the scene of the robbery on foot, leading the mule. After freeing themselves (assuming they were ever tied to begin with), Peró, according to one report, walked to Cotani, where he sent a message about the robbery to officials at the Aramayo mines. An article in an Oruro newspaper called *La Prensa*, however, stated Peró hurried back to Uyuni to report the incident. Perhaps he did both.

From Ann Meadows's *Digging Up Butch and Sundance*, Peró is on record as stating the "two Yankees wore new, dark-red, thin-wale corduroy suits with narrow, soft-brimmed hats, the brims turned down in such as way that, with the bandannas tied behind their ears, only their eyes could be seen." One of the bandits was "thin and of normal stature," while the other was "heavyset and taller." Peró also said the robbery took place at 9:15 in the morning on November 4, 1908.

The Shootout

According to an eyewitness named Remigio Sanchez, two gringos arrived in San Vicente on November 7 from the east, one riding "a dark brown and the other on a solid black mule" (in Patterson's *Butch Cassidy: A Biography*). According to Sanchez, the "tall gringo was dressed in a light-brown cashmere suit, a grey hat, red gaiters, a belt with about twenty-eight bullets, a gold watch, a dagger, and a silk handkerchief. The smaller one wore a yellow suit, apparently cashmere, red gaiters, [and] a grey hat. . . . Both were unshaven blondes."

If the two men who rode into San Vicente were the same ones who robbed the Aramayo payroll three days earlier, they must have changed their suits. This is a possibility assuming they were transporting a change of clothes in their saddlebags. On the other hand, for two bandits on the run and traveling light, this seems somewhat improbable.

Furthermore, it seems odd that payroll-robbing bandits on the run, traveling back roads, and living in the woods, would be dressed in rather expensive cashmere clothes and wearing gaiters. Garments made of cashmere were normally reserved for special and formal occasions such as cotillions and corporate meetings, not riding on mules along the poor and dusty back roads of the Bolivian countryside.

According to Sanchez, the two men, after arriving in San Vicente, asked him about lodging, and he referred them at once to the residence of Bonifacio Casasolo. The residence was part of the local police station and also served as an inn when necessary, a not uncommon association in small South American towns where travelers were concerned about their possessions.

The two strangers were provided a room that opened onto a small courtyard surrounded by an adobe wall. A short time later, "the police inspector, with two soldiers and the corregidor," arrived at the room to learn the identities of the two newcomers. According to Sanchez, one of the four men, a soldier, passed though a gate, entered the courtyard, and approached the room in which the newcomers were eating and drinking. Suddenly, the smaller of the two, identified by some as Butch Cassidy, "appeared and fired one shot and then another." The soldier was struck and ran screaming to a nearby house, where he expired.

A somewhat different version of the encounter was described in an article in *La Prensa*, which stated that a "posse of policemen" caught up with the bandits at San Vicente. On seeing the policemen, according to the article, the bandits drew their pistols and "unleashed a veritable hail of bullets at their pursuers, who answered with a blaze of fire as if hunting wild animals." The gun battle was described as "intense . . . a tremendous din and the furious shouting of the bandits and the police were all that could be heard" (Patterson's *Butch Cassidy: A Biography*). The gun battle, according to the article, lasted for more than an hour, with the two bandits being killed, "their bodies riddled with bullets."

Another article, this one based on the notes of Percy Seibert, stated several patrols were sent out in pursuit of the gringo bandits shortly after the robbery occurred and that the supposed malefactors were captured in Salo, located a few miles north of Tupiza. In fact, in a November 5, 1908, letter, Peró wrote that two men—allegedly a North American named Ray Walters and an Englishman named Frank Murray—were both detained by Salo authorities. The two closely matched the descriptions of the bandits. Tupiza officials learned of the San Vicente shootout and the deaths of the two strangers three days after the event. A short time later, they provided for the release of Walters and Murray from their Salo confinement.

Who, exactly, were Walters and Murray? A few Cassidy researchers have wondered if the two men temporarily incarcerated at Salo were, in fact, Butch Cassidy and the Sundance Kid. Though Cassidy and Harry Longabaugh were never known to use the aliases "Walters" and "Murray," it is surprising that this aspect has never been thoroughly investigated. Walters and Murray remain a deep mystery to this day.

Yet another newspaper offered a different version of what transpired at San Vicente. The article stated that a military patrol traveled to San Vicente, where two North Americans were encountered. A ferocious gun battle ensued that lasted more than an hour. In the end, the two bandits and one soldier were killed. The same article also stated the Aramayo payroll robbery occurred on November 6 and the shootout took place on November 10.

A story related by the noted and intrepid explorer and archeologist Hiram Bingham III differed markedly from other accounts. Bingham came to Argentina on November 15, 1908, and learned from "reliable" sources that, approximately one week prior to his arrival, the bandits who robbed the Aramayo mine payroll were from Arizona and had been tracked by fifty Bolivian soldiers who ultimately surrounded the hut in which they were hiding. According to Bingham, the bandits killed "three or four of the soldiers" and wounded several more. The thatched roof of the hut in which they had taken refuge was set afire by the attacking forces, causing the bandits to flee into the open where they were shot down, "each with half a dozen bullets in his body" (in Patterson's *Butch Cassidy: A Biography*).

So far, the only thing consistent about what happened regarding the two strangers who arrived in San Vicente is the inconsistency with which the details were related.

Inconsistency and contradiction likewise make a positive identification of the strangers difficult to impossible. In addition, the actual number of attackers who surrounded the house of Casasolo and shot at the bandits varies dramatically with different reports, the numbers ranging from four to several dozen. Furthermore, some accounts say they were Bolivian soldiers, other accounts say they were Bolivian police, and yet another claims they were mostly San Vicente citizens.

In still another version of the incident appearing in Sucre's newspaper *La Manana*, four men—identified as Sheriff Timoteo Rios, Captain Justo P. Concha, and two soldiers—were in pursuit of the bandits and arrived in San Vicente around 8:00 p.m. on November 6 and, according to the article, confronted the strangers. If true, they must have waited at least a day to do so since most reliable accounts have the strangers arriving on the afternoon of November 7. Additionally, if the newspaper account is to be believed, it means the strangers rode into San Vicente after the arrival of the small posse. In any case, as the article continued, one of the newcomers shot and killed a soldier, initiating a half-hour gun battle in which the gringos were killed. Captain Concha stated in a letter dated November 7 that the two bandits, along with one soldier, were killed.

Even more accounts surfaced, one volunteered by a Walter Gutierrez, who is considered by some an authority on the holdup and the shootout. Gutierrez claims the bandits arrived at San Vicente around 7:00 p.m. and were approached by fifteen to twenty soldiers. There was no shootout says Gutierrez, none of the soldiers were killed, and the bandits simply surrendered. Moments after surrendering, they were shot and killed by the soldiers.

There is more. Another account claimed that when the bandits were approached by the soldiers, they tossed the payroll money onto the patio. As the soldiers examined the contents of the packs, the outlaws escaped through the thatched roof.

Yet another version of what happened at San Vicente comes from a man named Froilan Risso. Interviewed by Meadows (in *Digging Up Butch and Sundance*), Risso claimed his father, ten years old at the time, witnessed the shootout. Risso stated the two strangers were in a room that opened onto a patio when "twenty soldiers" approached.

One soldier, Victor Torres, passed through the patio gate and was immediately shot by one of the outlaws. The soldiers started firing back. According to Risso, "everybody was firing their guns [and the] noise was incredible." Following the gun battle, which lasted until nightfall, said Risso, the two gringos were killed.

The San Vicente corregidor, Cleto Bellot, also submitted a report, which Meadows includes in *Digging Up Butch and Sundance*. He wrote that the two Americans arrived on November 6, the same day he had been advised that the Aramayo payroll shipment had been robbed. As Bellot was walking toward his home, he noticed the newcomers stop at the home of Casasolo. Bellot approached the strangers, and they asked him about lodging and fodder for their mounts. Casasolo appeared moments later, and Bellot told him to provide both.

According to Bellot, the strangers unsaddled their mules and placed their gear and rifles in the courtyard. Afterward, they retired to the room where Bellot joined them. The pair asked Bellot directions to Santa Catalina, Uyuni, and Oruro.

Bellot left and went directly to see someone he called the "commission inspector" and informed him of the arrival of the two strangers. The inspector, along with Bellot and two soldiers, procured rifles, loaded them, and carried them when they went to Casasolo's house and entered the courtyard. Apparently the newcomers did not like the sight of the Bolivians approaching their room with weapons, and one of them appeared in the door with a pistol and shot one of the soldiers, a man named Victor Torres. As Torres fell, he fired a shot and the other soldier fired two shots. While the wounded Torres was scrambling away, Bellot fled, and the second soldier took up a position in a doorway and shot at the Americans from there. The inspector, according to Bellot, also fired his rifle at the strangers.

Following the confrontation, continued Bellot, Captain Concha appeared, said he needed help, and requested he be assigned some men. Bellot went out and recruited some townsmen. As he was rounding up volunteers, Bellot claimed in his report he heard "three screams of desperation" from inside the room of the Americans. When the volunteers arrived, Captain Concha positioned them around the home. Following that, no more shots were fired save for one by the inspector around midnight.

According to Bellot, several men entered the room at 6:00 a.m. in the morning of the following day and found the two gringos dead, one in the doorway and the other on a bench.

According to Bellot, Concha's role was limited to requesting backup and then standing around observing. The evidence, according to Meadows's husband, Dan Buck, appears to suggest the two men in the room were essentially opposed by the Uyuni police inspector and one soldier. In other words, the two strangers lodging in the room faced at least two, and at the most four, potential adversaries. Captain Concha was apparently not directly involved in the alleged gun battle, and there were not, in spite of reports to the contrary, dozens of Bolivian soldiers involved.

The odds facing the two strangers at San Vicente that November 7 evening would surely not have been daunting to the likes of Butch Cassidy and the Sundance Kid, experienced outlaws who had been outnumbered numerous times during their bandit careers.

Ultimately, the account of Cleto Bellot, who was at the scene, varies considerably from that of Arthur Chapman, who was not. In truth, there is little consistency in any of the numerous reports.

Even more confusion is heaped upon the already contradictory accounts relative to the possessions of the dead men. As San Vicente officials inventoried and listed the belongings of the two, it was learned that the tall stranger had in his possession a Winchester carbine along with 121 cartridges. Elsewhere, 149 cartridges were reported. If true, how does one account for the stories that this same individual raced from the room into the courtyard in order to retrieve weapons and ammunition?

A second contradiction is that only one saddle was found, although Bellot earlier reported that both men were seen unsaddling their mules and placed their "saddles" on the floor of the courtyard.

Yet another problem arose. One of the men, the one many believe was Butch Cassidy, was initially identified as "Enrique B. Hutcheon" based on seven business cards bearing that name found on his person.

Who was Enrique B. Hutcheon? Did such a person exist, or could this have been a new alias for Cassidy? Some have suggested this was so, but there has been no supporting evidence. As a result of more research by Meadows, it was learned from the family of James "Santiago" Hutcheon, the man who employed Cassidy and Longabaugh shortly after the two left the Concordia Tin Mines, that Enrique B. Hutcheon "might have been James' half-brother" but that Enrique denied any knowledge of his involvement in the Aramayo robbery or the incident at San Vicente. Since James Hutcheon was a well-respected businessman, it is likely the family would deny such a thing.

The notion has been advanced that Enrique B. Hutcheon was half Chilean. This observation is relevant in light of subsequent discoveries by Meadows. For years following the San Vicente incident, it was commonly related around the town that one of the strangers killed and buried in the cemetery was a Chilean. Furthermore, reports of a number of robberies that took place in South America that supposedly involved Butch Cassidy and the Sundance Kid revealed that at least one of the participants was a Chilean.

THE BURIAL

Author Richard Patterson writes that, according to Victor Hampton, who worked in the mines near San Vicente during the 1920s, and who obtained his information from an Aramayo manager named Roberts, the two dead strangers were taken to an Indian cemetery not far away and buried on the same day they were found dead. This account, or versions of it, is the one popularly accepted relative to the disposition of the bodies of the victims. As with the robbery and the so-called shootout, even this event is fraught with contradiction.

Froilan Risso claimed the two strangers were buried in the village cemetery during the afternoon following their deaths. He stated the bodies were not placed in coffins but instead "flung into an open grave in the cemetery" (in Patterson's *Butch Cassidy: A Biography*).

Risso led Meadows to the San Vicente cemetery and showed her the grave in which he claimed the two strangers were buried. Pointing to a "small, fissured, concrete monument wedged between two large and relatively new slabs," he stated that "it used to have a cross on top and plaque engraved with words" (in *Digging Up Butch and Sundance*). Risso said the single grave contained both of the bandits. In spite of Risso's description, another San Vicente resident claimed there never was any plaque.

A Dr. Oscar Llano Serpa stated he had evidence there was never any registration of the location of the so-called grave of the bandits, and as a result, today it would be "impossible to be certain of exactly where it is."

Meadows was told by a cemetery guard that the locals did not bury outlaws, that the bodies would have been dragged out onto the plains and left for scavengers. Meadows, in fact, encountered more claims that the graves of the two outlaws were unmarked, but one Francisco

Avila stated he had once seen a marker over the bandits' graves in the San Vicente cemetery.

On November 20, Carlos Peró, along with his son Mariano and his servant Gil Gonzalez, came to San Vicente. They had been invited to identify the bodies of the two dead strangers as the pair who robbed the payroll. Shortly after the arrival of the trio, the bodies were exhumed. After examining them, Peró stated that he possessed "not a shred of doubt" that the payroll robbers and the victims were the same (in Meadows's *Digging Up Butch and Sundance*). Peró expressed not a shred of doubt even though he admitted earlier that all he ever actually saw of the robbers were their eyes.

During an interview with the magistrate, Peró explained that he recognized both men, "as well as the hats they wore, with the exception of their clothing, which is different from what they wore [earlier]." Peró also stated that the mule taken from the bandits was the same as the one taken "from me at the scene of the robbery."

Meadows expressed some concern with Peró's statement, noting that the mule he identified was not at San Vicente at the time of his visit but rather at Uyuni. How was Peró able to identify the mule if it wasn't there? This casts even more doubt on Peró's entire statement and identification and generates some serious concerns over his already questionable credibility. Could Peró, in fact, have been looking at the cadavers of two men entirely different from those who robbed him two weeks earlier? Given the nuances of his testimony, it is probable.

A thorough evaluation of the newspaper accounts and testimony of participants and observers pertinent to the so-called San Vicente shootout reveal that they often differ dramatically, are quite inconsistent, and in several cases, even contradict one another. Given the already obvious confusion as to what actually happened, compounded by the passage of so much time, the truth of the San Vicente events remains muddled and quite elusive.

A summary examination of the evidence identifies the inconsistencies and confusion, and simply leads to additional questions and conundrums:

1. There exists no substantial evidence whatsoever that would lead one to believe conclusively the robbery of the Aramayo mine

payroll was conducted by Butch Cassidy and Harry Longabaugh. The evidence that suggests those two men were involved in the robbery is circumstantial at best. Furthermore, after examining all of the statements by robbery victim Carlos Peró, it is easy to conclude that no one knows exactly what transpired during the robbery, since statements, explanations, and identifications attributed to the courier are conflicting and contradictory.

2. The two men who rode into San Vicente three days following the Aramayo holdup were wearing clothes markedly different from the garb worn by the robbers. It seems unlikely that two bandits, making haste to leave the scene of the crime far ahead of real and potential pursuit, would be carrying extra suits, especially expensive suits of cashmere—possible, perhaps, but not very likely.
3. Who exactly were Ray Walters and Frank Murray, the two men who resembled the Aramayo bandits and who were detained briefly by the Salo police before being released? Why were they not investigated? Could they have been aliases employed by Butch Cassidy and the Sundance Kid? This represents a major conundrum and could be significant to this case.
4. There is little or no agreement on which day the two strangers arrived in San Vicente. Some reports say November 6; others say November 7. The time of day they arrived is also in question. Furthermore, the day the so-called shootout took place has been identified by most as November 7 and by others as November 10.
5. There is no agreement on whether the South Americans involved in the so-called shootout were soldiers, police, or citizens, or combinations thereof. Furthermore, there is no agreement on how many Bolivians were involved in the confrontation—the numbers range from two to several dozen.
6. Based on different reports, there is no complete agreement on whether the strangers to San Vicente were killed during a gun battle, committed suicide, surrendered and were then shot, or escaped.
7. Reports also differ on whether a full-fledged gun battle was waged or only a few shots fired. Estimates range from three shots to hundreds.
8. The duration of the alleged gun battle is not agreed upon: estimates range from approximately one minute to over an hour. One researcher, Kerry Ross Boren, claims the gun battle never occurred at all. In support of Boren's oft-challenged claim is a

former Bolivian president, Rene Barrientos. Barrientos assigned an investigation team to study the events associated with the San Vicente incident: residents of the town were questioned, corpses were exhumed, and military and village records were examined. Barrientos concluded that the entire event was a fabrication.

9. The time of day given for when Casasolo's room was entered and the dead strangers discovered is listed as 6:00 a.m. in one report and noon in another.
10. There has never been a positive and conclusive identification made of the two strangers killed in San Vicente. A September 30, 1910, document that originated in Tupiza stated that, in spite of an investigation, no one could learn the names of the two "North Americans" killed at San Vicente. A subsequent communication from the same source mentions that a death certificate for the two gringos does not exist. The initial identification of one of the dead men as Enrique B. Hutcheon, perhaps a half-Chilean, casts even more doubt on the likelihood that the strangers were Butch Cassidy and Harry Longabaugh. This information, coupled with news reports that one of the bandits in a series of holdups attributed to Cassidy and Longabaugh was identified as a Chilean, only adds to the already abundant confusion. Ultimately, the two dead men who were buried in the San Vicente cemetery were not identified. It was only twenty-two years later that, as a result of Arthur Chapman's contrived article, most believed the two men were Butch Cassidy and the Sundance Kid.
11. Long after the deaths of the strangers in San Vicente, newspapers in the area continued to carry reports that Butch Cassidy and Harry Longabaugh, probably accompanied by Harvey Logan, were still committing robberies in the area as late as 1910.
12. In 1914, the Pinkertons received an unverified report that Butch Cassidy had been arrested in Antofogasta, Chile, on a charge of murder. Given the above contradictions, it would be extremely difficult to conclude that Butch Cassidy met his end at the small South American village of San Vicente in November 1908.

There are other contradictions, ones related to the personality and recorded experiences of the outlaw Butch Cassidy, the way he operated relative to his profession of outlawry, and the manner in which he reacted and responded to pressure and pursuit from law enforcement authorities. Given what has been oft documented about this famous bandit, one can only conclude that the behavior of the San Vicente stranger some have identified as Cassidy was completely out of character for the outlaw. The reactions and response of the shorter of the two strangers exhibited a pattern of behavior quite the opposite of what one would come to expect from Butch Cassidy, as in the following examples:

1. According to witnesses, the stranger identified by some as Cassidy, on seeing the approach of a man toward the room in which he had taken temporary residence, pulled his revolver and shot and killed him. This purely contradicts the long-standing and well-documented behavior of Butch Cassidy. Not only did Cassidy never harm a robbery victim, but also he was known to chastise members of his gang for doing so. The notion that the real Butch Cassidy pulled a pistol and shot a man before even learning of his intentions is inconsistent, and to some, unthinkable.
2. It was likewise out of character for Cassidy, if indeed he was fleeing from a payroll robbery, to stop and spend the night in a town or village. Based on previous accounts of his robberies, the likelihood is greater that he would have traveled the back roads and stayed as far away from settlements as possible.
3. The statement of Cleto Bellot that the strangers placed their saddles and rifles on the patio and retired to their room, if true, strongly suggests these November visitors to San Vicente were not Cassidy and Longabaugh. Given their previous experiences with posses, and realizing they were most certainly being pursued, it would have been highly unlikely for them to have carelessly left their weapons so far away.
4. The notion that Cassidy shot his companion Longabaugh and then turned the gun on himself is far fetched. Not only is the killing of his friend and partner, as well as suicide, out of character for him, but also to have done so in the face of odds of four to two is ridiculous. After all, here is a man who confronted, fought, and outfoxed dozens, if not hundreds, of lawmen throughout much of America's frontier West. Is this the kind of man who would kill himself when faced by four men, perhaps only one of which was a professional lawman? Hardly.

Based on the above, no one knows what happened in San Vicente, nor is there any evidence that Butch Cassidy and Harry Longabaugh were among the participants.

The only potential evidence that might determine whether or not Butch Cassidy and the Sundance Kid were the victims of the San Vicente "shootout" lay in the nearby cemetery.

Convinced by what many would argue is the sparest and most contradictory of evidence that Cassidy and Longabaugh were killed and buried at San Vicente, Meadows determined the best, and perhaps only, way to settle the problem once and for all was to have the bodies exhumed and subjected to an analysis. After making the decision to do so, Meadows was confronted with a number of obstacles—physical, cultural, and legal—but she dealt with the problems like a determined and seasoned professional researcher, eventually overcoming or evading most of them.

Faced with conflicting information relative to the actual graves of the two strangers killed in the San Vicente incident, Meadows eventually located what she believed, marker or no, to be the site at which the strangers were buried.

The evidence for which she had been searching theoretically could lay only a few feet below the surface.

FIFTEEN

Exhumation

Assuming that Butch Cassidy and the Sundance Kid met their end in San Vicente as a result of being confronted by law enforcement authorities or soldiers, and assuming their bodies were buried in the nearby San Vicente cemetery as many claim, then it should be an easy thing to dig up their remains, subject them to analysis, identify them, make a final determination about what actually happened, and put the matter to rest. This is precisely what researcher Ann Meadows had in mind. If the remains of the two men proved to be Butch Cassidy and the Sundance Kid, the controversy over whether or not one, the other, or both died in San Vicente or survived and possibly returned to the United States would forevermore be over.

Once the bodies are exhumed, the investigator would be in the position of initially determining whether or not the bodies were those of two North American Caucasians. One of the bodies, if it belonged to Butch Cassidy, would be approximately five feet eight to five feet nine inches tall and would have weighed about 165 to 170 pounds in life. It would also possess blond hair and a light complexion. Scars and other marks that could be used for identifying the Cassidy corpse would include two small cuts on the back of the head, a small red scar under the left eye, a red mark on the left side of the neck, and a small brown mole on the calf.

The other corpse, if it belonged to Harry Longabaugh, would be five feet nine inches to six feet tall and would have weighed 165 to 190 pounds in life. Longabaugh features would include light brown hair with a slightly reddish tinge, a long Grecian-shaped nose, and according to family members and Pinkerton records, the distinct possibility of a bullet wound in the left leg.

As Meadows embarked on the exhumation project, she was told by a San Vicente resident that, as outlaws, the two men would have likely been wrapped in blankets and interred vertically or face down in the grave as a sign of disrespect. The residents, he said, would not have wasted a coffin on common outlaws.

Following a series of delays and obstacles, Meadows and her group finally received permission to dig in the cemetery. One of those assisting her was Clyde Snow, a forensic anthropologist who made a reputation for himself identifying the bones of Josef Mengele, the noted Nazi war criminal. Snow, as it turned out, was working on a project in Brazil when he learned about Meadows's research.

Shortly after the excavation of the gravesite was begun, one of the diggers enlisted by Meadows had penetrated several feet into the hard earth of the cemetery when he ascertained that whoever was buried at this location had, in fact, been placed in a coffin and laid horizontally, not vertically. Furthermore, the body had apparently been buried face up. Already, this discovery departed from what the team was led to expect.

Once the body—actually a skeleton—had been located, the excavation became more meticulous and careful. For the most part, the wood of the coffin had rotted away and the bones had to be removed from a matrix of dirt. Early in the excavation, a mandible (jawbone) was found. Snow identified the mandible as belonging to a male approximately the same age Cassidy and Longabaugh would have been in 1908. The mandible contained three gold teeth, the result, according to Snow, of "high-quality dental work" (in *Digging Up Butch and Sundance*).

For the rest of the day, the bones of the deceased were removed from the grave and brought to the surface—ribs, scapulae, humerus, and vertebrae. When the diggers finally reached the bottom of the coffin, they were eight feet below the surface. By the time it was deemed prudent to cease the excavation, only one body had been found where everyone believed there would be two. Among the bones and dirt, the diggers also found a buckle, a button, and a pair of small boots. The discovery of the small boots was initially promising, for it was known that the Sundance Kid had small feet.

The skull that was taken from the grave was closely examined. It was described as being long and narrow and clearly not belonging to Cassidy but possibly resembling one that might fit Longabaugh. The forehead of the skull between the eyes was shattered, and Snow claimed the wound was "consistent with the damage from a gunshot wound at close range." The alleged wound was also consistent with the description provided by witnesses relative to what happened to the taller of the two strangers involved in the shooting. Additionally, minute copper fragments, possibly from a bullet, were also found in the bone of the skull.

Oddly, there was no exit wound, something one might expect assuming the victim was shot at close range. Snow also declared the wound was most likely inflicted by someone other than the deceased. "Had it been suicide," Snow determined, "the wound would likely have been in the temple or upper mouth."

Witnesses to the San Vicente shooting also claimed the taller stranger had been struck by bullets several times in the arm, but none of the radii, ulnae, or humeri bore any evidence of wounds. It is possible that, had the victim been shot in the arm, the bullets passed through flesh without ever striking bone.

Assuming the excavation was conducted, as initially believed, at the site where the two strangers were buried, it was indeed puzzling that the remains of only a single individual was found. At this point, most investigators would have deduced that the location was probably not the burial site of the two presumed bandits if, as had been reported, they had been tossed into a single grave. However, based on what scanty evidence was available, Meadows's group initially and optimistically concluded that the bones they found *might* have belonged to Harry Longabaugh. It was certain they did not belong to Butch Cassidy. Thus, as a result of the preliminary analysis and a process of crude deduction, the team seemed anxious to believe it was in the possession of the bones of the Sundance Kid, although not those of Butch Cassidy.

Continued examination of the skeleton was necessary to establish a stronger link between the body and the Sundance Kid. Closer analysis was at first promising for it revealed a gunshot wound on the left tibia, a bone in the lower leg. The wound was an old one, one suffered many years before interment, and it more or less matched the one the Sundance Kid was alleged to have.

Regarding the three gold teeth found in the skull, a Pinkerton report states that, as a result of an interview with Lillie Davis, who married Will Carver, Longabaugh "used to have a gold tooth in front, [on the] left side . . . [but he] had it taken out" and replaced with a white one (in Meadows's *Digging Up Butch and Sundance*). However, the report was several years old. If the bones belonged to the Sundance Kid, he might have had additional dental work done during one of his trips to the United States with Etta Place.

The bones tentatively identified as belonging to the Sundance Kid were eventually taken to a house in San Vicente and arranged on a table. Following a more detailed examination of the remains, Snow pronounced the decedent was "pretty definitely Caucasoid," a male who stood between five feet eight to six feet two inches in height. Thus far, the number of similarities between the skeleton and Harry Longabaugh seemed to be growing and afforded some encouragement.

In order to achieve a positive relationship, a DNA comparison test was suggested. For the basic DNA test to be valid, the investigators required genetic material from a maternal Longabaugh descendant. Unfortunately, none could be identified. A refined DNA test was recommended, one that could use DNA material from a paternal descendent, of which there were several. The test was conducted, and when the results arrived they clearly showed the bones were not those of the Sundance Kid. Just to be on the safe side, a DNA test was also conducted with Cassidy relatives. Again, as expected, there was no match.

Still attempting to establish a connection between the exhumed bones and the Sundance Kid, Snow gave the skull to one Lewis Sadler, a man who, according to Meadows, "pioneered a technique in which digitized photographs of people are superimposed over video images of skulls in order to determine whether they match at certain points." At a laboratory at the Department of Biomedical Visualization, University of Illinois at Chicago, Sadler, employing tissue-depth markers on the skull, reconstructed an outline of the head as it might have looked if it had flesh attached to it. Following the procedure, one of Sadler's associates called Meadows to inform her that it was a match—the skull, he claimed, belonged to the Sundance Kid.

The conclusion was premature and without basis. In spite of Meadows's contention, Sadler did not pioneer any such photoanalysis techniques. At least two court-approved and statistically valid photo-comparison methods had been in use and available long before this time, and it is curious that Sadler did not employ them. Sadler's technique lacks any kind of statistical validity, a primary requirement in a scientific study. However, Sadler was apparently impressed enough with the results of his project to go to the press and tell them he was "convinced" the skull belonged to the Sundance Kid. In the meantime, Sadler's associate issued a statement saying the analysis was inconclusive.

Sadler, it should be pointed out, employed his computer technique to "prove" a man named William Henry Roberts was not Billy the Kid. Like the Sundance Kid project, Sadler's Billy the Kid study, while impressing a handful of hobbyists and some outlaw history buffs, possessed no scientific validity and was roundly rejected by experts. Sadler's so-called computer studies as they relate to identification have been described by facial-comparison experts as being more along the lines of a classroom project rather than a scientific study and are not regarded credible by professional and qualified investigators.

A second burial site was eventually discovered near the first one. Encouraged that Butch Cassidy may still be found, the team continued digging. From the new excavation came the remains of a wooden coffin and several bones, including two skulls! Snow identified one of the skulls as belonging to an Indian, which eliminated Cassidy. On the other hand, it must be recalled here that "Enrique B. Hutcheon" was the identity initially attached to one of the dead men at San Vicente and that subsequent investigation suggested Hutcheon was half Chilean. Could this have been Hutcheon's skull?

According to Snow, a portion of the cranium of the second skull manifested evidence of "entrance and exit wounds in the temples" that, according to the investigators, matches witnesses' descriptions of the condition of the shorter San Vicente stranger believed by some to be Butch Cassidy. This skull appeared promising and invited additional analysis.

Weeks later, a portion of the second skull was powdered so DNA could be extracted. When the DNA sample was compared to those taken from relatives of Butch Cassidy, however, no match was found. Finding no DNA match does not completely eliminate the possibility that the skull belonged to Cassidy, but continued analysis of the fragments by Snow yielded the conclusion that it, like the earlier one, was not Caucasian and therefore could not possibly have belonged to the outlaw.

As a result of the efforts of Meadows and her group, they determined that the two skeletons exhumed from the site believed to contain the remains of the two presumed bandits who died at San Vicente in November 1908 did not to belong to either Butch Cassidy or Harry Longabaugh.

Could they, then, belong to two men who were mistaken for the famous North American outlaws? If so, it would be a simple thing to conclude that Cassidy and Longabaugh did not, in fact, perish at San Vicente. At this point of the quest, the possibility is great.

As a result of a later comparison of two-decades-old photographs of the cemetery, however, it was eventually determined that Meadows's team had dug up the remains of a man named Gustav Zimmer, a German miner who once lived and worked in the area.

In spite of the negative DNA analysis, the fact that two of the skulls found belonged to Indians, the discovery that the first gravesite was that of Gustav Zimmer, and bits and pieces of other evidence, it remains surprising that many are still convinced the two men alleged to be the robbers of the Aramayo mine payroll were killed in San Vicente and buried in that same cemetery. Whether or not the two men were Butch Cassidy and the Sundance Kid was now open to even more conjecture than previously, with logic and reasoning tilting dramatically toward the distinct possibility they were not. The evidence that Cassidy and Longabaugh were killed at San Vicente was growing even more flimsy.

According to Meadows's own research and analysis, the body exhumed was most certainly not that of Butch Cassidy and only has the remotest chance of being Harry Longabaugh. The likelihood that it belonged to Gustav Zimmer was considerably greater.

The question remains: where are the bodies of the two strangers killed in November 1908? Could they, in fact, have been hauled out onto the plains as was earlier suggested by a resident?

Despite some compelling evidence otherwise, Meadows and her husband in 1996 somehow remained convinced that the two men killed in San Vicente were Butch Cassidy and the Sundance Kid, that they were buried in the town's cemetery, and that they are still there, or nearby, in an unmarked grave yet to be found.

Clyde Snow, on the other hand, was quoted as saying he was certain they had the correct gravesite to begin with and that they simply needed to excavate deeper. It is inconceivable, however, that in 1908 the San Vicente residents would have dug a grave for two presumed outlaws in excess of eight feet.

In spite of Meadows's extremely important and significant discoveries relative to the South American activities of Butch Cassidy and the

Sundance Kid, as well as her important efforts to locate and evaluate the burial site, she has not uncovered any conclusive, or even substantial, evidence that Cassidy and Longabaugh were (1) guilty of robbing the Aramayo payroll, (2) killed in San Vicente in November 1908, or (3) buried in the San Vicente cemetery.

So, once again the question must be asked: what happened to Butch Cassidy?

SIXTEEN

Return of the Outlaw, Butch Cassidy

Following the alleged gun battle at San Vicente and, according to many, the subsequent deaths of Butch Cassidy and the Sundance Kid, rumors abounded that the two outlaws—specifically Cassidy—were still alive. In fact, the initial death reports, or more precisely, death rumors, were met with considerable skepticism, not only among the Parker family and friends of Butch Cassidy, but among the Pinkertons as well. During the time of the so-called shootout in San Vicente, the Pinkertons probably knew more about the location and activities of Cassidy and Harry Longabaugh than anyone. A thorough search of the files of the Pinkerton National Detective Agency yields no information to suggest they ever believed Butch Cassidy had been killed in San Vicente.

According to several sources, many weeks, perhaps months, after Cassidy's alleged death, a number of Cassidy's friends—including Matt Warner, J. K. W. Bracken, Bert Charter, Elzy Lay, and Charley Gibbons—collected some money and sent a man named Walker to Bolivia to ascertain the truth about the outlaw's reported death. When Walker returned, he said that, after interviewing several soldiers and San Vicente residents, he determined the story of Cassidy's death was true. Walker reportedly returned with a photograph of the corpses of Cassidy and Longabaugh.

On examining the photograph, however, Bracken claimed the body identified by some as Cassidy was actually that of an outlaw named Tom Dilly.

Following the appearance of Arthur Chapman's article in 1930, a number of Butch Cassidy's friends stepped forward to dispute the assertion that the outlaw was dead. Many of them stated they had visited Cassidy during the years since the alleged San Vicente shootout.

Since the "deaths" of Cassidy and Longabaugh in 1908, dozens of reports surfaced either stating or implying they were still alive, several of them issued by the Pinkerton National Detective Agency. The two famous outlaws were reportedly seen not only in South America but also in Mexico and in the United States, time and again, and over a period of the next three decades.

As members of the Parker family went about their lives in Utah, they occasionally heard rumors that Butch Cassidy was still alive and had been seen in various locations in South America, as well as in the United States. Lula Parker Betenson claimed her father was certain Cassidy was alive, but the family never understood how he knew.

For the three decades following the incident at San Vicente, a man believed by many to be Butch Cassidy appeared on numerous occasions throughout parts of the American West. He visited extensively with members of the Parker family and with many known friends of Butch Cassidy. Who was this man? Was it really Butch Cassidy, or was the return of this famous outlaw merely a hoax? An examination of the events relating to his appearances offers some rather stunning revelations, as well as some compelling evidence that continues to baffle researchers.

The first recorded mention of seeing the outlaw Butch Cassidy in the United States following his departure to South America in 1901 actually occurred prior to his alleged death in San Vicente. The year was 1906, and the sighting occurred in Ogden, Utah.

According to Betenson, a young man named Pete Parker, who knew Cassidy well, used to deliver messages between the outlaw and his lawyer, Douglas A. Preston, when the outlaw was on the run in Wyoming and Utah. Betenson once received a letter from the son of Pete Parker in which an encounter between his father and Butch Cassidy was described.

Pete Parker arrived in Ogden one afternoon in 1906 to take a train that would carry him to college in Logan. Since the train was not leaving until the next morning, Parker checked into a hotel. On the way to his room, Parker noticed a man sitting in the lobby who looked familiar to him. Stunned, Parker suddenly realized it was Butch Cassidy. He and Cassidy spoke for approximately forty-five minutes, during which time the outlaw asked Parker about his parents and neighbors.

The following morning, Parker went down to the desk to check out and discovered that Cassidy had paid his hotel bill and left him a package containing two brand-new white shirts. In the pocket of one of the shirts was a $20 gold piece. Following the visit with Parker, Cassidy supposedly returned to the mines in Bolivia. If the incident is true, it verifies that Butch Cassidy returned to the United States for a time during his residence in South America, probably accompanying Harry Longabaugh and Etta Place during one of their trips.

Jim Gass and Butch Cassidy were boyhood friends in Circleville. Gass once told Cassidy's sister, Lula Parker Betenson, about an incident wherein he and Butch once found a fawn pinned to the ground by a fallen log, one of its legs apparently broken. Gass suggested they shoot the fawn to put it out of its misery. Butch, however, was determined to save the animal. After freeing the deer from under the log, Butch splinted the leg and the fawn was able to walk.

Gass once said of Cassidy that he couldn't kill a dog, let alone a man.

Sometime during the year 1908, Gass returned from a trip to California. He immediately went to visit Betenson and informed her he had seen her brother, Butch Cassidy, at the train station in Los Angeles. According to Gass, the two men spotted each other at the same time and both waved. Butch's train pulled away before they could speak.

It was unclear whether Gass's sighting of Cassidy occurred before or after the alleged San Vicente shootout.

The first clear sighting of Butch Cassidy after the San Vicente shooting occurred in Mexico. During the Mexican Revolution, an Anglo family named Bowman was living in Colonia Juárez, a Mormon colony in the Mexican state of Chihuahua located in the foothills of the Sierra Madres. Here, they became acquainted with Butch Cassidy in 1910. According to Betenson, Henry Bowman had been taken prisoner by the federal soldiers and was about to be executed when Cassidy interceded. Mrs. Bowman said Cassidy agreed to provide the *federales* some information on the whereabouts of Pancho Villa on the condition that Bowman be released. The Bowmans took a picture of Cassidy, and years later, the photograph was presented as a gift to Betenson.

The Bowmans later moved to Texas and eventually raised horses on a farm not far from El Paso. According to Mrs. Bowman, Butch Cassidy arrived at the farm one day and remained a guest for several weeks. Finally, she said, he returned to Mexico.

Author Larry Pointer secured a revealing interview with Fred Hillman. Hillman, it will be recalled, was the young man Butch Cassidy frightened with a snake while he was working on his father's ranch in Wyoming's Big Horn Mountains; this was in 1897, following the Castle Gate payroll robbery. According to Hillman, he was returning to his house from working in the hay fields one afternoon when he spied a man standing under a tree in the front yard, apparently waiting for him. Hillman walked up to him, and the stranger smiled and asked how the hay crop was doing. After exchanging pleasantries for a few minutes, the stranger grinned at Hillman and asked, "Have you had any rattlesnakes tossed up on the hay rack with you lately?" (according to Pointer). At that point, Hillman realized he was talking with the man who worked for his father for a time, the ranch hand who befriended him when he was a thirteen-year-old youth, the man who taught him how to shoot, and the man who, it was later discovered, was the outlaw Butch Cassidy.

Joseph Claude Marsters worked as a horse wrangler for Cassidy and Longabaugh in South America and knew the two men well. In 1915, Marsters had a job riding bulls with a traveling Wild West show. During a performance in San Francisco, Marsters was walking back to the chute following a ride when a cowhand walked up to him and told him that his old boss thought his riding had improved since he had last seen him. The cowboy pointed to the "old boss" up in the stands, and when Marsters turned to look, he saw Butch Cassidy waving at him.

In 1922, a stranger drove a Model T Ford into John Taylor's Rock Springs garage for some repairs. While Taylor was working on the car, the stranger asked him a lot of questions about current and past residents of the town. "He didn't tell me who he was," wrote Taylor, "but I recognized [Butch Cassidy]" (according to Pointer).

In 1924, Cassidy allegedly visited an old friend named Tom Welch near Green River, Wyoming. According to Welch, Cassidy was driving a Model T Ford and pulling behind it a small, two-wheeled trailer containing camping gear.

Tom Vernon was a well-known citizen of Baggs, Wyoming, often referred to as "Mayor," although the town was too small to support such an office. As a young man, Vernon knew Butch Cassidy and often played music at Baggs dances attended by members of the Wild Bunch. According to Vernon, Butch Cassidy returned to Baggs "sometime in the twenties" and stayed with him for two days (in Patterson's *Butch Cassidy: A Biography*). The two men relived a number of events and adventures from the old times. Vernon said he never had any doubt that the man who visited was Cassidy.

In 1925, according to writer Pointer, a visitor camped for several weeks in a grove of trees not far from the Charter Ranch near Jackson, Wyoming. According to Boyd Charter, the seventeen-year-old son of the owner, the stranger remained mostly to himself but eventually became acquainted with the boy. Pointer interviewed Boyd Charter in 1973 and learned that the youngster overheard his father tell a friend named Will Simpson that the man camped nearby was Butch Cassidy. Simpson was the prosecuting attorney who was, in part, responsible for Cassidy being sent to prison in 1894.

According to Crawford MacKnight (a nephew of Ann Bassett), his family, including Ann, was camping in Nevada mining country some fifty miles east of Las Vegas. MacKnight said a man named "Masson" arrived at their camp one afternoon and spent a great deal of time visiting and talking with Ann. MacKnight said the man never told Ann who he was but commented that he had known her well when the two of them were much younger and living in Brown's Park. He told her he had eaten many dinners at the Bassett home. All of a sudden, said MacKnight, Ann recognized "Masson" as Butch Cassidy. Later, Ann took some photographs of Cassidy. MacKnight claimed the photographs of "Masson" closely resembled images of Butch Cassidy.

Ann Bassett made a second trip to the region to visit Cassidy in 1928. Accompanying her was her niece, Edith Jensen, and her nephew and his wife, also named Edith.

According to writer John Rolfe Burroughs, Josephine Bassett Morris met with Butch Cassidy near Rock Springs, Wyoming, sometime during the 1920s. It is alleged by a number of Cassidy researchers that Josephine Bassett was once Cassidy's sweetheart. Josephine Bassett Morris moved to Rock Springs when her sons were old enough to attend high school.

One afternoon, Morris related, Butch Cassidy and Elzy Lay entered a Rock Springs saloon and visited with the bartender, a man named Bert Kraft, whom they had known years earlier. Kraft told the two men that Josephine was living nearby. At Cassidy's insistence, Kraft called her and made arrangements for Cassidy and Lay to come to her home. Their visit extended well into the night as the three, according to Morris, relived old times.

According to writers Dick and Daun DeJournette, Josie Bassett Morris met with Cassidy two more times in 1928, once in Baggs, Wyoming, and once again in Johnnie, Nevada. Morris claimed Cassidy passed away sometime in the 1940s, in Johnnie.

Johnnie, Nevada, figures prominently in another Butch Cassidy story. Johnnie was the site of a rich gold mine, discovered sometime during the early 1900s. The Johnnie mine was an active producer of gold between 1908 and 1940, at which time it was finally shut down.

A number of stories emanated from the Johnnie mine, stories that Cassidy worked there for a time. Some of the stories claim he was a mining engineer, others say he was merely a night watchman. A few researchers concur with Josie Bassett Morris's statement that Butch Cassidy died in the small town. Writer Edward M. Kirby investigated the potential Johnnie, Nevada, connection with Cassidy and, in the process, encountered a longtime resident named Fred Cook. Cook maintained Cassidy lived in Johnnie from 1930 to the mid-1940s. Cook even showed Kirby a gravesite he claimed was that of the outlaw. A wooden cross over the grave bore the name "Bill Kloth."

A dramatic return of Butch Cassidy to his family was detailed by Lula Parker Betenson in her book, *Butch Cassidy, My Brother*. It occurred one day in 1925. Lula Parker was forty-one years old. The family was living in town, but on this day her brothers were all out in the field working with the stock and repairing fences.

Mark Parker, one of Butch Cassidy's brothers, was working on a fence near the road when a brand-new black Ford described as a touring car pulled up. After a moment a man got out and stood by the car looking at Mark. Initially, Mark thought it was a cattle buyer named Fred Levi, a cousin, who had stopped by to talk about a purchase. As the man stepped into the field and approached Mark, however, he stopped working on the fence and stared into the face of the stranger. Suddenly, Mark realized it was his own long-lost brother, Robert LeRoy Parker, alias Butch Cassidy. Cassidy would have been fifty-nine years old.

The two men embraced, and there was much hugging and backslapping. They visited for about thirty minutes and then climbed into the car and drove to town.

Betenson recalls that, when the Ford pulled up to the family house in Circleville, Maximillian Parker, the father, was sitting in the sun on a step just outside the kitchen door. He was eighty-one years old, possessed a shock of white hair, and "wore a thick, white mustache." Betenson described her father as "a fine-looking man, straight and alert, and . . . dressed immaculately."

The Ford pulled to a halt, and Mark stepped out from the passenger side, much to the surprise of the elder Parker. Mark had left for the ranch earlier that morning on horseback. As Mark stood by the car, grinning, the driver stepped out and rose to his full height. Old man Parker stared at him, wondering who he was.

Butch Cassidy remained next to the Ford, his heart beating heavily. For over four decades he had stayed away from his family for fear that his presence would bring them shame, that they would be ostracized by their neighbors because they had brought an outlaw into the world. He had not seen his family for over forty years, and this moment was filled with a certain terror for him. He wondered if he should simply get back in the car and drive away.

In spite of his fears, Cassidy grinned at his father, and Maxi Parker immediately recognized his first son. The two men embraced for a long time, and with tears in their eyes, they entered the house.

Lula Parker Betenson had been preparing dinner when Mark entered the kitchen and told her to fix an extra plate, that they had company. After setting out the plates and the food on the kitchen table, she stepped into the living room and eyed the stranger. On seeing her, the newcomer rose. As she studied his face, she thought he looked familiar but could not ever remember meeting him before. From his features, Lula deduced he must be a relative of some kind.

At that moment, the elder Parker said, "Lula, this is LeRoy." Years later, Betenson related she was stunned that this was her famous brother standing before her. Though she was certain, as a result of family comments, that Butch Cassidy was still alive and was living in the United States, she never anticipated meeting him.

As the family sat in the living room and visited that evening, according to Betenson, Butch Cassidy spoke most of all about his late mother. His heart was heavy with regret for the pain and humiliation he believed he caused her. He felt certain he had disappointed her and broken her heart.

Cassidy described in detail that morning in 1884 when he left home and how his mother, holding Dash, the family dog, watched him ride away. He described the blue blanket she had given him and the food wrapped inside it. He told of riding past the poplar trees alongside the road and recalled how he helped his mother plant them after the family hauled them all the way from Beaver.

Later that evening, Cassidy related tales about South America, about how he and the Sundance Kid went down there to straighten out their lives and find honest work. He talked about the constant pursuit and persecution from the Pinkerton detectives. "When a man gets down," Betenson quoted him, "they won't let him up."

Cassidy said that, sometime after the alleged gun battle at San Vicente, he and Longabaugh separated and planned on returning to the United States. They were going to rendezvous at a certain location, but Cassidy suffered a severe scorpion sting and his leg became so swollen he could not travel. For several weeks, his wound was treated by an Indian woman, and he missed the meeting with the Sundance Kid.

Eventually, Cassidy traveled northward, spending some time in Mexico working at various jobs. One afternoon he was relaxing in a local tavern when he felt a hand on his shoulder. Fearing he had been identified, he experienced a brief moment of fear. When he turned around, however, he looked into the face of Etta Place! She and Longabaugh happened to be staying in the same town, and she invited him to come and stay with them. After two days, Cassidy left the pair and had not seen them since.

After leaving Mexico, Cassidy said he traveled to Alaska where he trapped and prospected for a time. He found the weather unsuitable there and returned to warmer latitudes, eventually settling in the Pacific Northwest, where he remained for a while. He found the state of Washington agreed with him, fell in love with the region, and eventually decided to make it his permanent home. He told his family that, after visiting them, he would return to Washington where he intended to live out the rest of his life.

Cassidy remained with his family for two days. After leaving them, he traveled to other parts of the region, searched for, located, and spent another week visiting with his brothers. Finally, he left to return to the Pacific Northwest. He requested his family not tell anyone he was alive or that he had come to Utah to see them. They agreed to keep his visit a secret. After returning to Washington, he wrote a number of letters to his father. According to Betenson, Butch Cassidy never returned to Utah.

During Cassidy's visit to his family, he told them he had led a completely honest life since 1909. He also stated that, after it was reported he had been killed in Bolivia, he wanted very badly to return home but was afraid of bringing shame to the family he loved so much.

Many of Cassidy's relatives and friends knew he had not been killed in South America and that he was still alive during the 1920s and 1930s. They kept the secret. In letters to Lula Parker Betenson, and via interviews conducted by others, many of them recalled meeting and visiting with Cassidy during his return trips.

In a letter to Betenson, a man named W. H. Boedeker wrote that Butch Cassidy visited Dubois and Lander, Wyoming, in 1929. According to the letter, Boedeker's father, Henry E. Boedeker, and Cassidy became acquainted during the late 1880s when the former was hauling lumber. The two, in fact, roomed together at Lander's Cottage Home Hotel. It will also be remembered that, at the time Cassidy was arrested for horse theft, Lander constable Henry Boedeker was one of the lawmen who accompanied the prisoner to the jail at Laramie. According to W. H. Boedeker, he was operating the Frontier Cafe in Dubois in 1929 when three men entered the establishment and ordered meals. One of the men began asking Boedeker questions about his father and others who once lived in the area. Before the conversation was finished the man admitted to being Butch Cassidy.

According to a Mrs. Jess Chamberlin of Arapahoe, Wyoming, Butch Cassidy joined her husband and father-in-law on a camping and fishing trip in 1933. During the trip, said Chamberlin, Cassidy searched for and found a cache of money he had buried almost fifty years earlier.

According to a man named William G. Johnson, Butch Cassidy, while visiting Lander in 1934, purchased some groceries from a Harry Baldwin who owned a store there. According to Pointer, after remaining in and around Lander for a while, Johnson said Cassidy left to return to "his home in Seattle, Washington, where he is known as William T. Phillips." Johnson also commented that Cassidy was suffering from cancer of the stomach and was not expected to live much longer.

Larry Pointer wrote that Tacetta B. Walker, a Lander resident, was told in 1936 that Butch Cassidy had returned to the town to visit friends about two years earlier. Walker wrote that several Lander old-timers recognized the outlaw, and one old fellow stated that he talked about things only Butch Cassidy would know.

At one point during his visit, Cassidy encountered the son of a banker he had known years earlier. On seeing and recognizing Cassidy, the son embraced him. During their subsequent conversation, he called him "George" and "Cassidy."

In 1934, Butch Cassidy also visited his old friend Eugenio Amoretti, the banker who helped him out with the Horse Creek Ranch he and Al Hainer started.

It is also believed that Cassidy visited his old girlfriend Dora Lamorreaux during his 1934 visit to Lander, but details of the encounter are unknown.

While in Lander, Cassidy asked his old friend Will Boyd to arrange a pack trip into the Wind River Mountains. This was done, and a comfortable camp was set up for an extended stay. Daily, Cassidy ranged far from camp and was occasionally observed digging around the stumps of old trees. It is believed by many he was searching for some loot he cached following one of his robberies.

While Cassidy was staying in the camp, Will Boyd decided to surprise him. Without telling anyone, he sent Roy Jones to bring Mary Boyd out to the camp. Mary and Cassidy were lovers at one time during the early 1890s, and it is believed they planned to get married. On arriving in camp, Mary, at the time a widow, and Cassidy recognized each other immediately, and they spent long hours together during the next few days reliving past times.

During the succeeding months, Mary Boyd received several letters from Cassidy, all postmarked from Spokane, Washington. In 1937, he sent her a ring set with a Mexican fire opal. The ring was inscribed:

Geo C to Mary B

When Boyd and Cassidy were lovers, the outlaw was using the name George.

Lula Parker Betenson claimed her brother passed away in 1937. One day that year, Maximillian Parker received a letter from a man named Jeff who informed him that his son, Robert LeRoy Parker, alias Butch Cassidy, had died of pneumonia. Jeff informed the family he had attended to arrangements for burial. The location of the gravesite remains a Parker family secret to this day.

During the late 1960s, Lula Parker Betenson began writing a book about the return of her brother. Some claim she was influenced by the popular 1969 movie *Butch Cassidy and the Sundance Kid*, starring Paul Newman and Robert Redford. Others insist she started her book before the movie was released. By 1970, her manuscript was still not published—she claimed she had been turned down by several publishers because she refused to reveal when and where Butch Cassidy had died and was buried.

Eventually, in 1975, an academic press—Brigham Young University Press in Provo, Utah—published the book. The publication remained popular for a long time and enjoyed decent sales for an academic press product. And, as normally happens when someone writes and publishes something that contradicts or conflicts with prevalent thought and the historical status quo, the book, *Butch Cassidy, My Brother*, generated considerable criticism.

The vast majority of Betenson's detractors provided little in the way of substantial or even compelling commentary, but here and there some pertinent questions were raised relative to the accuracy of the contents of the book.

One of her principal detractors was Jim Dullenty who, around the time book came out, was the editor of a pulp magazine called *True West* that published material on things Western—outlaws, lawmen, lost mines, and so on. *True West*, while occasionally printing something that smacks of competent research, was never a credible historical publication, had no peer review process, and seldom troubled with fact checking. It was often sold in the "hobby" sections of some magazine racks, and the credibility and reliability of its content has often been questioned by qualified and credentialed researchers.

Dullenty, himself a man of some status in the field of Western outlaw research, openly expressed doubt about the accuracy and veracity of the Betenson book and claimed some of her own relatives manifested concern over the accuracy of the contents. According to Pointer, Dullenty was once quoted as stating that Betenson's book was "worthless," and that it "would have been better if she had not written it." It must be pointed out here that Dullenty was, at the time, working on his own book about Butch Cassidy.

Regarding the Betenson book, a few have expressed the notion that the sister was simply trying to cash in on the growing popularity of the outlaws. Dan Buck, the husband of Ann Meadows, is quoted in Meadows's book as saying, "Her claim that Butch told her Percy Seibert had deliberately misidentified the bodies so that his pals could come home without worrying about the Pinkertons proves she made the whole thing up."

In truth, Betenson's claim proves no such thing. It is difficult to imagine Buck making such a statement and causes one to question his own qualifications. Buck was also quoted as saying that Lula's son, Mark Betenson, "told us Butch didn't come back," as if such a statement carried any credibility whatsoever. It has been suggested that Buck may have disclaimed Betenson's book, in part, because she once offered some criticism relative to the notion that the exhumation process, in which he was involved, was not conducted correctly.

In fact, Betenson's grandson, Bill Betenson, maintains Lula was telling the truth but that several members of the family did not want her to write the book because of a promise made to Maximillian Parker.

In spite of Betenson's claim that her brother, Butch Cassidy, passed away in 1937, there were reports of additional appearances of the outlaw beyond that time.

Matt Warner and Butch Cassidy had been close friends for years. In conjunction with Murray E. King, Warner wrote in his biography *The Last of the Bandit Riders* (1940) that Cassidy and Longabaugh had indeed been killed by soldiers in San Vicente. It is likely that Warner was simply reporting what he heard, or perhaps what he read in Arthur Chapman's exaggerated account. Although Warner expressed the belief that it was completely unlike Butch Cassidy to commit suicide, the old outlaw appeared resigned to the notion that his longtime friend had been killed in South America.

According to Warner's daughter, Joyce, however, the old man changed his mind a short time before he died, insisting that Cassidy must have survived the encounter with the Bolivian soldiers. Joyce Warner related that her father believed up until the time of his death that his friend Butch Cassidy would come to visit him.

Joyce Warner related another rather provocative incident, one reported by writer Steve Lacy, an amazing tale that was published in 1982. She claimed that sometime in November 1939, almost a year after the death of her father, an elderly stranger came to her home asking for Warner. She told him her father had passed away. The visitor then asked her if Warner ever talked about a man named Butch Cassidy. The two engaged in conversation, and the stranger related accounts of his longtime friendship with Matt Warner, including how they once robbed a bank. The stranger's version of the bank robbery was identical to the one her father related. He also told her of some of his adventures in South America.

After visiting with the man for a while, Joyce Warner looked him in the eye and said, "You're Butch Cassidy, aren't you?" The old man admitted he was.

Joyce Warner also related that, for several months following the visit of the man she believed to be Butch Cassidy, she received letters from him. In 1941, she said, the letters stopped coming, and she presumed he had died.

Two issues of the *Salt Lake City Tribune* that appeared in October 1993 related another potential encounter with Butch Cassidy, this one occurring in 1941. In July of that year, a Utah state trooper named Merrill Johnson pulled over an elderly man for running a stop sign near Kanab. The old fellow was from out of state—the car bore California license plates—and Johnson simply wrote the driver a warning citation and allowed him to proceed on his way.

Trooper Johnson was living with his in-laws during this time, a family named Kitchen. That evening when Johnson returned home, he noticed the same car with the California plates that had been driven by the old man was parked nearby. When Johnson walked into the house, he was surprised to see the same old fellow visiting with his father-in-law, John Kitchen. Kitchen introduced the old-timer to Johnson as an "old friend of the family, Bob Parker—Butch Cassidy." Johnson recalled during the conversation that evening that the old fellow talked quite a bit about his life in Bolivia. Kitchen and Cassidy had known each other years earlier in Utah.

The following day, Trooper Johnson drove the old man to Fredonia, Arizona, where he met with Bill Parker, whom he said was his brother. After driving him back to Kanab, the old man drove away, telling Kitchen he was on his way to Wyoming.

Merrill Johnson was not particularly well versed in Western outlaw history, and so the name Butch Cassidy did not leave him as impressed as some others would have been. Later, when Johnson was showed photographs of the outlaw Butch Cassidy, he stated there was no question they were images of the same man who visited father-in-law in 1941.

The accounts from people who claimed to have been contacted by Butch Cassidy years, decades, after he was supposedly killed in San Vicente, Bolivia, are numerous and compelling. What are the chances that Cassidy lived past 1908 and returned to the United States? Since no conclusive evidence exists that Cassidy was killed in San Vicente, or anywhere else for that matter, the possibility remains great.

It would be helpful to subject the post-1908 encounters with Butch Cassidy to close examination and attempt to provide some explanation. Consider the possibilities of what may have occurred:

1. The events involving the return of the outlaw Butch Cassidy were lies. Several researchers have contended that the alleged meetings and visits with Butch Cassidy during the first four decades of the 1900s were contrived, made up, and that those who reported such things had lied.

2. An imposter assumed a Butch Cassidy identity. Some have expressed the notion that someone posing as Butch Cassidy may have visited the Parker family and other Cassidy haunts and friends, passing himself off as the famous outlaw.
3. Butch Cassidy survived the South American experience and did, indeed, return to the United States. A number of researchers are convinced the outlaw Butch Cassidy did, in fact, live beyond 1908 and return to the United States, where he passed away as an old man.

Regarding the first possibility, it is difficult to believe, even for the most cynical, that dozens of people during a period of over three or more decades and separated by great expanses of geography could or would manufacture tales of encountering Butch Cassidy in the United States, meetings that exhibited some consistency relative to dates and places. While the chances that some of those who reported visits from Cassidy could have been exaggerated, many more were credible, honest individuals who stood nothing to gain from making up such a story. Even if only one of the dozens of those who claimed to have seen Cassidy was correct, that is enough to cause one to consider such a circumstance.

The second possibility—that someone assumed a Butch Cassidy identity and managed to fool Cassidy relatives and friends—is hardly worth considering. That someone posing as Cassidy, someone who looked remarkably like the outlaw, managed to pass himself off and succeed in fooling all of those people, most of whom knew Cassidy well or were related to him, and would certainly not be duped by an imposter, is not only highly unlikely but also preposterous.

The third possibility—that Butch Cassidy did return—likewise presents problems. While the evidence that such a thing happened is plentiful and, in many cases, complementary, there is no absolute and uncontested proof. All researchers have to rely on, for the most part, are eyewitness accounts and a few photographs. The photographs, while suggesting that Butch Cassidy did indeed return, do not represent hard, uncontested evidence. However plausible, however likely Butch Cassidy did return following his alleged death in San Vicente, Bolivia, it has never been proven beyond the shadow of a doubt.

Into this mix of theory and speculation about the return of Butch Cassidy arrives a man named William T. Phillips, believed by many to be the final alias for the outlaw.

SEVENTTEN

Enter William T. Phillips

The last time Butch Cassidy was officially heard from was via a February 16, 1908, letter he wrote to Clement Rolla Glass in La Paz from the Concordia Tin Mines. Following that date, there exists no verification, or even substantial evidence, that Butch Cassidy remained in South America.

Three months later, a man named William T. Phillips appeared in the United States. Years later, when Phillips was investigated, it was discovered there existed no documents to prove that he ever existed prior to 1908. In other words, shortly after Cassidy disappeared, Phillips appeared.

Many of those who reported encounters with Butch Cassidy in the United States after he was allegedly killed in Bolivia stated that the outlaw often used the alias "William T. Phillips."

So, who exactly was William T. Phillips? Where did he come from? Why is his life prior to May 1908 unaccounted? And, more importantly, could he possibly have been the outlaw Butch Cassidy?

Most of what is known about this rather enigmatic man whom many believe was the famous outlaw has come from the extensive research of two men—author Larry Pointer and magazine editor Jim Dullenty.

When Pointer was married in Lander, Wyoming, in 1972, one of the members of the wedding party was a man named Allan Robertson, a grandson of Dora Lamorreaux. Lamorreaux was one of Butch Cassidy's sweethearts during the early 1890s. From Robertson's father, Bill, Pointer heard a number of stories about Cassidy returning to Lander to visit friends during the 1930s, tales often related by the late Lamorreaux.

Intrigued by this information that severely contradicted generally accepted history, Pointer undertook a study of Butch Cassidy, all the while pondering the possibilities that the outlaw survived the Bolivian shootout and came back to the United States. During the course of his research, Pointer encountered James Dullenty, at the time a reporter for a Spokane, Washington, newspaper. Dullenty, who knew about William T. Phillips, had written a series of intriguing articles about him for his newspaper. Together, Pointer and Dullenty pursued additional research into the possibility Phillips could have been Butch Cassidy. Eventually, however, the two men fell into disagreement and went their separate ways, each of them independently pursuing their own research agenda, and both making significant contributions relative to William T. Phillips.

Logically, Pointer decided to begin investigating Phillips with his date and place of birth and trace him from that point on. Almost immediately, however, contradictions arose. When Phillips passed away in 1937, his death certificate placed his date of birth at June 22, 1865, in Michigan. His father was identified as L. J. Phillips and his mother Celia Mudge Phillips. Other Spokane records located by Pointer specifically identified Phillips's place of birth as Sandusky, Michigan, and his father's first name as Laddie. Given this beginning, Pointer made his way to Michigan to learn more.

Census records for Michigan during the middle of the nineteenth century were, relative to the times, comparatively up to date, complete, well ordered, and appropriately archived. Therefore, there should have been no trouble locating Phillips's parents and his birth record. According to the Michigan records, however, no such person as Laddie J. Phillips ever existed. A Celia Mudge was located, but her recorded date of birth would have placed her at only twelve years old when giving birth to William T. Phillips. Furthermore, the records show Celia Mudge was married in 1875 to one Hezekiah Snell. According to Pointer, descendants of the Mudge-Snell union never heard of William T. Phillips.

Further research into Phillips's past yielded no information whatsoever. The first legitimate paperwork ever associated with the man known as William T. Phillips was dated May 14,1908—his marriage license. On that date, he was wed to Gertrude Livesay in Adrian, Michigan. Prior to that date, there is no evidence that Phillips ever existed under that name.

Phillips had come to Adrian, he told people, to get away from the hustle and bustle of Des Moines, Iowa, to relax a bit and see the country. While walking through the streets of Adrian, Phillips once related, he wandered into a church where he met his future wife, who was visiting from nearby Morenci where she lived.

Gertrude Livesay was described as "plain" and "sickly." She suffered from chronic asthma and remained generally weak most of the time. She was thirty-two years old when she married Phillips. The wedding occurred following a rather brief courtship and in direct opposition of the wishes of her mother and sister. Gertrude's father had been dead for five years at the time. On the marriage license, Phillips recorded his name as William Thadeus Phillips, his age as thirty-four, and his residence as Des Moines. He claimed he had been born in Michigan and his profession was "mechanical engineer." Following a honeymoon in Colorado, the two moved to Globe, Arizona.

While living in Globe, it is entirely possible that Phillips joined a group of mercenaries organized to travel to Mexico and fight with the revolutionaries. The group of sharpshooters, called the *Falange de los Extranjeros*, was under the command of Captain Linderfelt, and each was paid six dollars per day. It was during this time that Henry Bowman claimed he encountered Butch Cassidy in Colonia Juárez in the Mexican state of Chihuahua.

Apparently the dry, high-altitude southwestern climate of Globe was beneficial to the asthmatic Gertrude Phillips, for she appeared to regain her health. During the late summer of 1910, the two traveled throughout much of Wyoming and Montana, eventually arriving in Spokane, Washington, in late December. It was during this trip that Phillips visited Dan Hillman and probably looked up old friend and former Wild Buncher Tom O'Day. Concerning O'Day, Phillips wrote the following in a manuscript several years later:

> All of the members of the original Wild bunch . . . except two had been wiped out. The one who had been most sought [had] now become a man of mystery and the man who he first met upon the day he entered the Hole in the wall, Tom O'day. O'day is yet living.

Indeed, according to the results of Pointer's research, Tom O'Day was, in fact, living at Lost Cabin, Wyoming, during the time Phillips claimed he came through.

Shortly after arriving in Spokane, Phillips took a job with the Washington Water Power Company. Following subsequent employment stints with something called the American Stereotypewriter Company and a prospecting trip to Alaska, Phillips started the Phillips Manufacturing Company (PMC) in 1915. The business of PMC, according to Pointer, was "the development of adding and listing machines." Pointer learned that the Burroughs Company was interested in Phillips's adding machine, apparently inviting the inventor to their corporate offices to discuss the matter. Phillips and the Burroughs Company could not agree on a price for the invention, and the inventor broke off discussion. Months later, Burroughs initiated production of an adding machine strikingly similar to the one designed by Phillips.

William and Gertrude Phillips were unable to have children, and in 1919 adopted a child, a boy named William Richard. They called him Billy.

In 1925, the Riblet Tramway Company, which had consigned work to Phillips Manufacturing Company on several occasions, asked the inventor to travel to Bolivia to manage the construction of a tramway. Phillips turned Riblet down but told Gertrude and young Billy that he was going to South America. Instead, he used this opportunity to travel to Wyoming and Utah. It was during the year 1925 that Butch Cassidy reportedly visited his relatives and many of his friends in those states.

Phillips eventually returned to Spokane and his business, which, at the time, was in solid, financial condition. Unfortunately, the Great Depression was approaching. One of Phillips's principal sources of income was the Riblet Tramway Company, but in 1928 it suffered severe losses and cut back significantly on its consignments. As a result, Phillips was, for all intents and purposes, out of work. In January 1929, he sold one-third interest in his company to his lawyer, Gardner L. Farnham. The agreement stipulated that if Farnham was unsatisfied with the deal within one year, Phillips would pay him back and regain his share. After ten months, Farnham asked for his money, but Phillips was so broke he was unable to pay it. In May 1930, Phillips's employees purchased the remaining shares. By June, Phillips offered to turn over the remaining one-third to them if they would assume all of his debts. They did.

Shortly afterward, Phillips returned to Wyoming, this time to hunt for stolen money reportedly buried by Butch Cassidy many years earlier. As far as is known, he never found any, and when he returned to Spokane, he was still broke. During the Depression years, Phillips worked at odd jobs where he could find them in Spokane, barely making enough money to keep food on the table. He was forced to sell his house and move into a more modest one in a less exclusive part of town.

In 1934, Phillips returned to Wyoming. On this trip he was accompanied by Ellen Harris and her son, Ben Fitzharris. Mr. and Mrs. Harris, living in Hollywood, California, at the time, had been neighbors and good friends of the Phillips family in Spokane. Mrs. Harris and Ben rendezvoused with Phillips in Salt Lake City and drove with him to Wyoming. Young Fitzharris had been told by his parents that Phillips was Butch Cassidy, but it made little impression on him at the time. On arriving in Wyoming and meeting so many of Cassidy's friends and listening to their stories, he quickly became convinced that the old man who was his traveling companion was indeed the former outlaw.

Young Fitzharris was dazzled by Phillips's exhibitions of marksmanship with Colt revolvers. According to Pointer, Fitzharris was quoted as saying Phillips was an "honorable man and a very powerful character, not only physically, but mentally powerful."

It was during this trip that Phillips was encouraged to write down the story of his life. When he returned to Spokane following his journey to Wyoming and Utah, Phillips began penning a manuscript he titled "The Bandit Invincible."

After Phillips's death, "The Bandit Invincible" was found. It is unclear whether the manuscript was intended to be a novel or a biography. According to Pointer, it was poorly organized, it was replete with misspellings, and there was no sense of order or chronology. A reading of numerous excerpts from the manuscript reveals no sense of composition style and a lack of intimacy with the construction and progress of such an undertaking. The manuscript also suggests a hurried attempt to record events of the past. Phillips wrote the manuscript, not as Butch Cassidy, but as a person who had known the outlaw from boyhood. For the most part, it was written as a third-person narrative, but in a couple of instances, Phillips slipped up and employed the first person.

In the preface of "The Bandit Invincible," Phillips wrote that much of what had been previously reported about Butch Cassidy had been conjecture and, for the most part, incorrect. He implied that he intended to tell the true story of the famous outlaw. In the first of what turned out to be many rationalizations of the outlaw's misdeeds, Phillips wrote that "Cassidy did not rob for the lust of gain, nor was it his natural trend. He had as he thought, every good reason for his first holdup, and after the first, there was no place to stop."

In the manuscript, Phillips purposely changed the names of people and places, possibly, as Pointer suggested, to protect those who were still alive or maybe even descendants of friends. Despite the purposeful changes, the chronological inaccuracies, and even perhaps some purposely misleading information, the manuscript, according to Pointer, carried "more truth than recorded history itself." Pointer claims "The Bandit Invincible" is "the last testament of a man who did wrong, who knew he did wrong, and who felt a need to tell others why he did wrong." It was Cassidy's way, suggests Pointer, to make peace with his maker.

Pointer undertook the enormous task of attempting to verify as much of the manuscript as possible. He traveled thousands of miles, spent countless hours in libraries, courthouses, reading newspaper files, and interviewing anyone and everyone who might have some insight into the life and activities of Butch Cassidy and the Wild Bunch.

Although the manuscript was written three to four decades after most of the events actually occurred, it contained descriptions of people and places that could only have been attained through personal experience. If William T. Phillips was not Butch Cassidy, he most certainly was with Cassidy when most of the events occurred, or at least not far behind him. Names and places included in the Phillips manuscript initially unknown to historians were researched and found to exist. If Phillips had not had firsthand experience, the only way he could have known certain specific details would have been to conduct thorough research in a number of small Wyoming newspapers that were in business during the late 1890s.

For example, in "The Bandit Invincible" Phillips mentions two Lander lawmen from the mid-1890s named Grimmett and Baldwin, two names not commonly found in the various histories of Butch Cassidy. However, Pointer examined the Fremont County, Wyoming, Sheriff's Record Book and found that a Sheriff Orson Grimmett served as Fremont County sheriff between 1895 and 1897, and from 1899 to 1901. Research in the pages of an 1890s issue of the Lander newspaper, the *Fremont Clipper*, yielded information on the activities of one Deputy Jim Baldwin. Dogged research by Pointer even turned up a photograph of a Lander saloon that existed only during the 1890s, a saloon that was referred to by Phillips in the manuscript.

Another example involved Phillips's mention of a location he referred to only as "Lone Bear's Village" near a bend in the Wind River. Subsequent research revealed that the Arapaho Indians, under a Chief Lone Bear, had been moved to the Wind River Reservation. "Only a person who had visited Lone Bear's village before [1906]," wrote Pointer, "could have described the Arapaho camp."

As with the two above, there were many other examples that strongly supported the contention that William Phillips was extremely intimate with this area during the time it was frequented by the outlaw, Butch Cassidy.

Concluding his examination and appraisal of the Phillips manuscript, Pointer determined it was "authentic . . . it is the autobiography of Butch Cassidy. The personal emotions and details from the outlaw's life could have been related by none other."

Additionally, Phillips included in his manuscript details about the life and times of Butch Cassidy in between robberies and other commonly recorded events, details that are absent from the historical record.

Many researchers are passionate about their belief that William T. Phillips and Butch Cassidy were one. Likewise, numerous skeptics are equally passionate about the notion that the two men could not have been the same.

No absolute proof exists for either contention, and much of the evidence offered in support of the conflicting claims is arguable and carries with it cadres of supporters and detractors.

For the contention that Butch Cassidy and William T. Phillips are the same man, we need an orderly and logical presentation of what is known, a critical evaluation of the evidence, and a deductive ratiocination based on that evidence.

The following chapter offers an analysis of what is known about Butch Cassidy and William T. Phillips.

EIGHTEEN

What Was the Fate of Butch Cassidy?

Despite the thousands of man-hours invested in the study of Butch Cassidy, the outlaw's life remains extremely cryptic and disputable. Even today, no one is entirely certain which train robberies and bank holdups Cassidy was involved in. It should be no surprise to anyone, therefore, that his death remains equally enigmatic and controversial.

Determining what actually happened to the outlaw Butch Cassidy is extremely difficult for a number of reasons. First of all, with the passage of a century, records and accounts of the day pertaining to Cassidy and related events are incomplete, if they existed in detail at all. It is fortunate, as well as fine testimony to the patience and perseverance of some conscientious researchers and investigators, that we possess as much information and knowledge about Cassidy and his life and times as we do. But regardless of what has been found and archived, the record remains astonishingly incomplete.

It is certainly easy to understand why the record is incomplete, particularly as it relates to his life from the time he fled from the United States to South America: Butch Cassidy was a wanted man intent on burying his past and pursuing a different kind of life. Purposely, he made his movements and activities throughout much of South America as secretive as possible. Save for employers and only a few acquaintances, he avoided and eluded any contact with the population at large. The reason is quite simple and quite apparent: while Butch Cassidy was on the run, he did not want to be found.

Second, regardless of whether we are willing to admit it or not, the 1969 William Goldman film *Butch Cassidy and the Sundance Kid* generated perceptions in the minds of the public that, though in most cases depart considerably from the truth, are nevertheless extremely difficult to dislodge. Even worse, many who presume to research and write about the history of Butch Cassidy, the Wild Bunch, and related topics, are often victims of these erroneous perceptions and are unable to distinguish truth from lore and fiction. As a result of their ultimate publications, many of these writers simply perpetuate and reinforce the popular, but often false, perceptions, rather than correcting them. This has been the case with numerous books and articles about American outlaws.

Third, a lot of the so-called research conducted in, along with the subsequent writing about, the field of Western outlaw history in general, and that pertaining to Butch Cassidy in particular, is performed not by qualified and credentialed historians and investigators but by hobbyists and history buffs. While a number of these hobbyists are competent writers, experience has proven time and again that their research methodology, if it exists at all, is lacking or questionable. Far too often, research to many of these enthusiasts amounts to little more than collecting and repeating information that has already been published.

The noted author Ramon Adams once stated,

> Nowhere has research been so inadequate or writing so careless as in the accounts of western outlaws and gunmen. Indeed, many chroniclers seem to delight in repeating early sensational and frequently untrue stories without any real attempt to investigate the facts.

In case after case, particularly as it relates to Butch Cassidy, very little in the way of truly professional research and sophisticated investigative technique accompanied by inductive and deductive analysis is ever undertaken.

There are several reasons for this. It has been suggested, and quite correctly, that the majority of competent and qualified historical researchers are employed by colleges and universities throughout the country. These individuals have been schooled in proper and effective research methodologies and, for the most part, can be regarded as experts in American history. Sadly, however, most colleges and universities do not regard Western outlaw history important enough to merit their time and attention. University scholars tend to pursue studies of a more universal orientation, and many academic institutions encourage or require their professors to devote their energies to matters perceived to be of greater import. Besides, studies in American outlaw history do not attract significant funding, and more and more university professors are under pressure to secure monies for their research activities.

Call it elitist, if you will, but outlaw history is just not ranked very high in importance among many of the nation's universities and their associated historians. Even those few qualified historians who do, in fact, spend some time pursuing outlaw studies too often know their subjects via the prevailing folklore and other discredited treatments. Additionally, legitimate professional and peer-reviewed publication outlets for such studies are rare.

Unfortunately for truth, much of the attention given to outlaw history has fallen into the hands of the enthusiasts, hobbyists, and history buffs, all good people, but people who generally possess little or nothing in the way of qualifications or credentials and who have limited knowledge of correct research methodology and technique. However pure their motives, they are largely responsible, as a result of incomplete and incorrect research accompanied by very little, if any, investigation and often very poor reporting, for clouding the historical truth. Many of them simply do not recognize the differences between hearsay and fact.

For most of them, the largest market for the publication of articles on their "research" is in pulp magazines that offer no peer review and questionable editing, and whose mission is less related to truth than it is to selling magazines. Another outlet for such writers has been the self-publishing or vanity publishing of books that have evaded all of the proper professional treatments any serious work demands and deserves. As a result, much of the so-called history of notable American outlaws such as Billy the Kid, Jesse James, and, of course, Butch Cassidy has evolved to a number of oft-repeated and unsubstantiated tales, and an absence of fact-checking, all of which help to further muddy the waters and cover the truth with an unnecessary sediment of error.

Poor chronicling and unsubstantiated research as it relates to Butch Cassidy began with Arthur Chapman's 1930 account of the San Vicente shootout. In 1938, Charles Kelly followed with his book *The Outlaw Trail*, which relied heavily on Chapman's version of events but contributed even more hearsay and lore disguised as fact. In 1941, George D. Hendricks released *The Bad Man of the West*, which perpetuated the growing mythology. James D. Horan included treatments of Butch Cassidy in four books, the first of which was published in 1949, the last in1976. Historian Frank Richard Prassel refers to Horan's books as "less than entirely reliable" and containing "numerous assumptions." Among a large number of amateur historians, the abovementioned books continue to be regarded as authoritative.

Fourth, there exists in the field of Western outlaw and lawman history a passion for the status quo, a certain reverence for things and events as they have long been thought to occur. Anything that challenges the prevailing thought, or more precisely the collective thinking of a cadre of self-appointed "experts," is commonly attacked, denigrated, and generally deemed unacceptable. Many of these so-called experts are not intimate with proper investigation techniques, are incapable of such themselves, and seem to resent it in others who choose not to align with them and other hobbyists and amateur outlaw historians.

For example, in 1998, I presented contemporary findings relative to the controversy over whether Billy the Kid survived the alleged shooting by Sheriff Pat Garrett in Fort Sumner, New Mexico, in 1881. Rather than enter into discussion or debate, Western lore enthusiasts who clung tightly to the historical status quo, many of whom were published in the aforementioned pulps, sent threatening letters and warnings. Because the status quo as it relates to the fate of Billy the Kid was threatened, those opposed to the premise bowed up and criticized the results of the study without ever once responding to an invitation to deliberate. The findings, all based on original research, competent investigation, state-of-the-art technology, and statistically valid analysis, were never responded to by the critics. When the hobbyists were invited to debate and have an opportunity to prove me in error on television, in newspapers, and in magazines, they never responded.

Humankind's view of history is never static. As more and more information becomes available, notions about what has happened often change, are modified, and are sometimes thrown out altogether. At one time in history, the idea of geocentrism—the earth is the center of the universe—ruled scientific thought. At one time in the not too distant past, the process of continental drift was believed to be embraced only by madmen. Today, examples of the reality and consequences of the shifting crustal plates are endless. It is no longer theory, as some would have you believe, but well-established, provable, scientific fact.

So it is with Western outlaw history. While many of these topics have been seemingly researched and written about as completely and thoroughly as can be expected, very few of them have, in truth, been investigated. The words *research* and *investigate* are often used interchangeably, and in many cases can overlap, but the latter, in the words of investigator Joe Nickell, "connotes a particular type of scholarly or scientific examination or inquiry." Applying this concept to historical investigation, Nickell defines it as "that aspect of research in which appropriate methodologies are applied toward the resolution of historical conundrums."

The goal of the investigator is the accumulation and development of proof sufficient to solve the problem. One important problem encountered here is that the standard of proof required to settle historical questions has never been codified. Clear and convincing evidence that leads to proof beyond a reasonable doubt is an extremely high standard that, unfortunately, generally remains impractical relative to historical questions and conundrums. This high standard is often forsaken for a lower one, one that simply relies on a preponderance of evidence.

When more than one hypothesis can account for the known, established facts, the one with the fewest assumptions is most likely correct. This principle is known as Occam's Razor, the "principle of parsimony," which essentially implies that the simplest explanation is usually the right one.

Butch Cassidy's alleged death and return is a historical conundrum, or more accurately, a set of historical conundrums. To solve this conundrum, we can only make analyses, inferences, and deductions using the existing evidence, and there is precious little substantial evidence. What evidence does exist, however, can provide some important direction toward solving the problem.

There are three events, or issues, relative to Butch Cassidy that must be explored pertinent to determining the fate of the outlaw. First, it must be ascertained whether or not he was involved in the robbery of the Aramayo payroll. Second, it must be determined whether or not it was Butch Cassidy who was involved in the San Vicente incident—the arrival, the so-called shootout, and the burial. And third, elements and evidence of the alleged return of Butch Cassidy must be evaluated.

Finally, given a thorough analysis infused with logic, inductive and deductive reasoning, and a dose of common sense, a conclusion can be made, a conclusion based on the amount and quality of the evidence, a conclusion invoking Occam's Razor.

The Robbery

There is little reason to doubt that a robbery of the Aramayo mine payroll occurred on or about November 4, 1908. The principal witness to the robbery was Carlos Peró, a mine official and the man in charge of escorting the payroll. However, Peró's identifications and descriptions remain suspect for they are entirely contradictory; thus, it would be dangerous to rely on his testimony that the robbers were Butch Cassidy and Harry Longabaugh. It would be useful if additional evidence existed that linked Cassidy and Longabaugh to the robbery, but there is none.

Researchers Ann Meadows and Dan Buck have offered what they interpret as additional evidence that Butch Cassidy and the Sundance Kid were guilty of the Aramayo payroll robbery: the memoirs of one A. G. Francis, a British mining engineer who was working in southern Bolivia at the time.

According to an article written by Francis and published in 1913, two men he "judged to be Americans" arrived at his camp sometime in August 1908. The strangers introduced themselves as Frank Smith and George Low and claimed they were stockmen on their way to Argentina. The three men enjoyed a fairly pleasant visit accompanied by friendly conversation during the next few days. Then, Smith and Low departed.

Francis encountered the same two men a second time in Tomahuaico, where he had later moved his operations—they rode into his camp only a few hours following the Aramayo robbery. According to Francis, one of the men described how they relieved Carlos Peró of the payroll money and fled.

The following day, an Indian arrived in camp to inform the three men that, in response to the robbery, a military detachment had been sent out and was on its way Tomahuaico. To Francis's dismay, his visitors asked him to guide them, telling him they were going to Uyuni.

Unwillingly, but not inclined to refuse, Francis guided the two men along a seldom-used route, finally arriving in the small village of Estarca, where they spent the night. In the morning, Smith and Low told Francis, much to his delight no doubt, that they were proceeding alone. That was the last Francis saw of the robbers. The next day, wrote Francis, he was informed that "two white men had been killed the previous evening at San Vicente."

While there is little doubt that A. G. Francis had an encounter with the two men who robbed the Aramayo mine payroll, there exists no credible evidence that either one of them was Butch Cassidy. Cassidy was never positively identified by Francis, and there is little to support the hypothesis that he was involved.

There is a serious problem associated with the presentation of Francis's recollections by Meadows and Buck as evidence of the involvement of Cassidy and Longabaugh in the robbery. In Meadows's book *Digging Up Butch and Sundance*, the author presumed to insert the names of Butch Cassidy and the Sundance Kid into Francis's narrative via brackets, leaving the reader with the impression that it was a foregone conclusion it was those two men and no others. Francis, in truth, never identified either of his visitors as Cassidy or Longabaugh. In fact, Francis offered a supposition that one of them was actually Harvey Logan. Meadows's and Buck's playing loose with Francis's words clouds, rather than clarifies, the real or hypothesized role of Butch Cassidy in the Aramayo payroll robbery.

In summary, despite a very remote possibility, *there is not a single shred of substantial or conclusive evidence that Butch Cassidy and Harry Longabaugh were the perpetrators of the Aramayo robbery.*

The San Vicente Incident

Here are the essential, generally accepted facts: two strangers arrived at San Vicente during the afternoon of November 7, 1908; the two were engaged in a confrontation with local authorities; and the two were killed, either by the attacking Bolivians or by their own hand.

From the available evidence, it appears that the two strangers were the same ones who robbed the Aramayo payroll, two men whose identities have never been positively determined.

So many different versions and interpretations of what transpired at San Vicente exist that it will probably never be possible to discover the truth of the principal elements of the events:

1. The exact day, as well as the time of day, the strangers arrived in San Vicente is not agreed upon.
2. The four Bolivians who approached the room in which the strangers took temporary residence have been identified in different accounts as either soldiers, policemen, civilians, or a "posse."
3. Their numbers have been reported to range from two to an entire company of armed soldiers.
4. The so-called gun battle has enjoyed a myriad of descriptions ranging from a couple of shots fired to a "veritable din, intense firing, lasting over an hour" (in Richard Patterson's *Butch Cassidy: A Biography*).

5. One researcher, as well as a former Bolivian president, claims no shootout ever occurred.
6. The dates of the shootout differ with different researchers.
7. Reports claim the strangers' rifles and ammunition were left in the patio, and other reports claim they were in the room with them.
8. Some reports state the strangers committed suicide, some say they surrendered, at least one says they were executed, and another says they escaped.
9. Some say the strangers were discovered dead at 6:00 a.m.; some say at noon.
10. Some claim the bodies were placed in a coffin; some say they were not.
11. Some claim the bodies were buried; some say they were not.
12. Some claim there was a monument placed over the graves; some say there was not.

In truth, no one actually knows what happened at San Vicente or who was killed.

Despite the acute paucity of substantial evidence, two arguments have remained prevalent regarding the San Vicente incident: (1) the two strangers who were killed were Butch Cassidy and the Sundance Kid, and (2) they were buried in the San Vicente cemetery.

Despite what many believe, despite the preponderance of the oft-repeated tales, and despite decades of research and investigation into the matter, there is no substantial, conclusive, or even compelling evidence that either Butch Cassidy or Harry Longabaugh were the two strangers who arrived in San Vicente, that they were killed in that town, or that they were buried in the local cemetery.

The Return of Butch Cassidy

Now for the major conundrum of the Butch Cassidy issue: did the famous outlaw survive his South American experiences to return to the United States, to visit family and friends, and to eventually die there?

The evidence in support of Cassidy's return is largely associated with the testimony of those family members and friends who claim he did. This evidence is relatively plentiful and, in the majority of cases, difficult to dispute. The only way it can be effectively challenged is to provide sufficient evidence that Cassidy was killed in Bolivia, or anywhere else for that matter, and that has never been done. Until more and better evidence is available to either confirm or contradict Cassidy's return, accepting the notion that he did relies on the aforementioned testimony of family and friends, along with a few photographs—all of which is evidence but not proof.

However, given the preponderance of this evidence, we are, deductively speaking, faced with the distinct possibility that Butch Cassidy did return.

The alleged return of Butch Cassidy is beset with a further conundrum: what was his identity in the United States after he came back? Clearly, it would not have been in his best interests to continue using the name Butch Cassidy, or even Robert LeRoy Parker. Logically, he would have adopted an alias. The prevailing thinking is that the alias and identity Cassidy employed was William T. Phillips.

A great deal is known about the man named William T. Phillips, at least as far as his life after 1908 is concerned. Previous to that, there is no record that he ever existed.

Phillips's life was reviewed in chapter 17, and it would serve no purpose to repeat it here. Essentially, however, we examine the prevailing arguments against and for William T. Phillips as Butch Cassidy.

Arguments against William T. Phillips as Butch Cassidy

Those who maintain the position that William T. Phillips could not have been Butch Cassidy offer as primary arguments the testimony of Phillips's wife, a computer analysis of the faces of the two men, contradictions of Lula Parker Betenson's claims her brother returned, and a handwriting analysis.

The Testimony of Gertrude Phillips

A year following the death of her husband, Mrs. William T. Phillips responded to a query from writer Charles Kelly, who was pursuing a potential link with Butch Cassidy. In the letter, printed in part in Larry Pointer's *In Search of Butch Cassidy*, Mrs. Phillips claimed her husband was "born and raised in an eastern state" and, influenced by dime novels, headed west. As a teenager, according to the letter, William Phillips "fell in with Cassidy" around the time of the Johnson County War. Gertrude Phillips said her husband knew Cassidy "very, very well." She also claimed she knew the outlaw as well.

As a result of the information contained in Gertrude Phillips's letter, Charles Kelly concluded that William Phillips only represented himself as Cassidy and used this assumed identity to search for buried loot. Phillips, claimed Kelly, was a fraud.

Based in large part on Gertrude Phillips's correspondence, Kelly's deduction is most often quoted by those who seek to dispute the claim that William T. Phillips was Butch Cassidy.

An examination of Gertrude Phillips, her personality, and her possible motives for making such a claim is necessary to provide a somewhat different point of view.

According to Pointer, Gertrude Livesay Phillips has been described as "shy," "withdrawn," "introverted," and "straight-laced." In Spokane, as William Phillips enjoyed the company of his several friends and neighbors, Gertrude became resentful and "embittered." The relationship between the two grew strained, and it was rumored that Phillips became involved in at least one extramarital affair. William Phillips, likely as a result of the tension generated by his declining income and the problems associated with his wife, began to drink more and more.

Between his depression and his drinking, Phillips's health declined markedly. When he became too great a burden to maintain at home, Gertrude finally had him placed in a nursing home. Once there, she never visited him. Gertrude Phillips passed away twenty-two years later in 1959.

William Richard Phillips, the adopted son of Gertrude and William T. Phillips, offers a different perspective relative to his mother's view that his father and Butch Cassidy were two different men. The younger Phillips told writer Jim Dullenty that, contrary to his mother's claims, his father was indeed Butch Cassidy and that the fact was well known in the Phillips family. His mother, however, preferred to say it was not true because she cared little for the associated notoriety.

Gertrude Phillips's testimony manifests at least three distinct elements that cause the investigator to question her credibility and veracity. First, she clearly cared very little about her husband during the last months of his life: once he was placed in a nursing home, she had nothing to do with him. The record shows that neighbors visited and saw to his welfare, but Gertrude did not. Second, her position on her husband as Butch Cassidy is contradicted by her own son. Third, her statement that she knew Butch Cassidy herself causes one to question her truthfulness: if, as she insisted, her husband was not Butch Cassidy, then how and where could she have possibly met the outlaw? The answer is most likely that she could not.

Ultimately, Gertrude Phillips's testimony that her husband, William T. Phillips, was not Butch Cassidy cannot be accepted as complete truth.

Photoanalysis

In 1991, a report of the results of a computerized photoanalysis was published in the pages of a pulp magazine called *Old West*. For comparison, the analyst, one Thomas G. Kyle, selected two photographs. One was the famous Wyoming Territorial Prison photograph of Butch Cassidy, a face-on view of a somewhat disheveled Butch Cassidy, a photograph that was taken on his admission to the facility when he was twenty-eight years of age. The other was an image of a besuited William T. Phillips, a photograph believed to have been made in 1930 when Phillips was judged to be in his mid-sixties. Though the ages of the subjects differ by greater than three decades, some similarities are initially evident in the eyes and noses.

In Kyle's analysis, the images are scanned and adjusted such that, according to the investigator, the distance between the eyes of each subject and the distance between the horizontal eye-distance line and the mouth are the same for both. The end result of this procedure is the superimposition of a grid over each face, a grid consisting of only two horizontal lines and two vertical lines.

With this grid in place, Kyle proceeds to analyze the ears ("somewhat different") and the noses ("do not appear quite similar"), even though those particular features are not in the least impacted by the grid. Kyle then states, "Hair and hairlines are also important landmarks in visual recognition" and concludes that the hairlines of the two men do not match, that Phillips's is lower than that of Cassidy.

Kyle then compares the sizes of the two men's heads by superimposing what amounts to crude outlines of each of their heads, one over the other, and "deleting all details but the edge of the hair and the profile of the head."

Kyle concludes his study stating that "Butch had a much larger head than Phillips, a telling comparison" and that Cassidy and Phillips were "different people." On the basis of the Kyle article, published under the title "Did Butch Cassidy Die in Spokane? Phillips Photo Fails," many have embraced the notion that the case on the Cassidy-Phillips connection is now closed. Kyle's analysis, however, begs to be criticized and consequently rejected—it fails on every point.

In the first place, it is bewildering to professional photoanalysts and researchers that Kyle employed such an elementary and error-prone nonstatistical analysis when at least two statistically valid procedures were available. The well-established Townes and Kaya-Kobayashi methods were procedures utilized regularly by the Federal Bureau of Investigation, the Central Intelligence Agency, Interpol, and progressive law enforcement agencies throughout the United States and the world.

In the second place, the design and methodology of Kyle's study was unsophisticated and without logic. The two images Kyle selected were clearly unsuitable for comparison: the Cassidy image is a full face-forward photograph that provides a bilaterally symmetrical head. The Phillips image, on the other hand, is that of a man whose face is turned a few degrees to his right, providing what professional photoanalysts call an "angled facial," which is rendered bilaterally asymmetrical and therefore not capable of being legitimately compared to the Cassidy photograph. Competent professional photoanalysts would never have considered undertaking a photo-comparison study employing these two photographs.

Kyle devoted a few sentences to his analysis of the subjects' ears. Ears, according to professional photoanalysts, are never used in facial photo-comparisons.

Even worse, while Kyle somewhat arbitrarily measures the distances between eyes and the eye line and mouth line, he completely omits the standard facial-comparison elements employed by professional photoanalysts, including internal biocular breadth, external biocular breadth, nose breadth, mouth breadth, bizygomatic breadth, midlip to chin distance, midlip to nose distance, and nose length.

Oddly, Kyle submitted the subjects' hairlines as evidence. Hairlines, like ears, state the professionals, are never used in professional photo-comparisons. Furthermore, even the most casual Butch Cassidy researcher knows that, for this particular photograph, the outlaw's hair was combed over a head wound in order to conceal it, thus disturbing, even camouflaging, the original hairline.

It should be pointed out that Kyle also conducted a similar photo-comparison study on Billy the Kid and a claimant, William Henry Roberts. The study was sponsored and commissioned by the Lincoln County Heritage Trust in a transparently biased attempt to perpetuate the historical status quo of Kid history in New Mexico. While embraced by hobbyists, Kyle's study was described as being replete with a "gross degree of error and misinterpretation" and that such an analysis "cannot be tolerated in any professional photo-comparison" (in my work *Billy the Kid: Beyond the Grave*).

Ultimately, not only was Kyle's study statistically invalid, but also the entire design and the methodology were illogical and unsound. Conclusions were drawn primarily on the basis of elements that are never included in professional facial photoanalyses. In short, it was completely meaningless.

As a result of the above considerations, Kyle's analysis cannot in the remotest sense be deemed acceptable and must be rejected. In truth, the Kyle photo study did not prove William T. Phillips was not Butch Cassidy.

Betenson's Claims Disputed

Those who would discredit the claims of Lula Parker Betenson that her brother, the outlaw Butch Cassidy, returned are quick to point to the notion that even her own relatives disagreed with her contentions and that her book, *Butch Cassidy, My Brother*, was even somewhat controversial among family members. Researcher Meadows levels mild criticism at the author, stating truthfully that Betenson "never provided any evidence to substantiate her stories" (in Meadows and Dan Buck's "Showdown at San Vicente"). Meadows's husband Buck is quoted as saying, "We've always thought Lula was just looking to cash in with that book of hers. If Butch had really survived, she would have had a livelier tale to tell."

Writer Dullenty has also been a severe critic of Betenson, pointing out that her story is filled with inconsistencies. Dullenty has also referred to an interview he once conducted with Max Parker, a nephew of Butch Cassidy, who stated that Betenson was not telling the truth and that events did not transpire as she related.

On the other hand, Betenson's grandson, Bill Betenson, stated the majority of the Parker family did not want her to write a book about their famous relative because of a family agreement never to reveal what actually happened. Regarding Betenson's book, the grandson said it told the complete truth.

Researcher Buck was quoted by author Richard Patterson as saying that "members of the Parker clan . . . have not gone on record in support of Lula's story" (in *Butch Cassidy: A Biography*). Given Bill Betenson's observation, it is easy to understand why many of them refused to do so. A greater truth is that, while some of the family did not support Betenson's contentions, a greater number were convinced Cassidy did return and that he used the alias William T. Phillips.

Ultimately, many of the criticisms leveled at Betenson's book have been shallow and without basis. Some appear to have been borne of jealousy, and a good many of them have never contained as much substance as the book itself.

It has also been argued by some Betenson critics that her book was not particularly well written or extensively researched. Yet, it is a book not of research but of her recollections, most of them stated as best as she remembered them, given the circumstances associated with the passage of time. True or false, they are her recollections. As far as the quality of writing is concerned, this book is an "as-told-to" publication, and the prose is the contribution of writer Dora Flack, not Lula Parker Betenson. Furthermore, until the past few years, academic presses such as the one that published Betenson's book have seldom been known for publishing good writing; rather, they are better known for academic treatments.

While harshly criticized by several whose motives for doing so are suspect, Betenson's recollections as recorded in her book, taken as a whole, are difficult to reject.

Handwriting Analysis

An oft-heard claim is that an analysis of the handwriting of Butch Cassidy and William T. Phillips proved they were two different men. The truth is somewhat different.

Author Pointer recorded that an authentic letter written by Cassidy in Argentina in 1902 was compared to a letter written by Phillips in 1935. The letters were given to Jeannine Zimmerman who was identified as a "legally certified handwriting expert."

In Zimmerman's final report, she offered the opinion "that both of the [letters] . . . were executed by the same individual."

In response to Zimmerman's report, Pointer wrote, "There can no longer be any question . . . William T. Phillips was Butch Cassidy."

It would not turn out to be quite that easy.

A Spokane newspaper employed its own handwriting analyst to re-examine the same two letters that had been submitted to Zimmerman. The second analyst, like the first, concluded that the letters might very well have been written by the same person. A third handwriting analyst, on the other hand, provided the opinion that the letters were not written by the same person.

Researcher Buck noted correctly that Zimmerman was a graphologist, not a forensic document analyst. Also, the other two opinions offered relative to the handwriting of the two men were likewise provided by graphologists. A graphologist uses handwriting to provide a personality profile. With reference to this, author Patterson quotes Buck as stating that graphologists "are not held in high regard among forensic document examiners" and that "their conclusions are open to question" (in *Butch Cassidy: A Biography*).

Pertinent to Buck's opinion on graphologists, a leading forensic handwriting analyst was consulted. Howard Chandler, a former state policeman and investigator, is recognized throughout the United States as an expert handwriting analyst, and his opinions, deductions, and court testimony are regularly sought, often in high-profile cases. Chandler stated the rift between forensic examiners and graphologists is not as wide as Buck implied and that representatives of the two specialties often work together to solve cases.

Regarding the handwriting samples of Phillips and Cassidy, no final decision has been made. The truth, as it relates to this issue, is that the handwriting analyses did not disprove Phillips and Cassidy were the same person. If anything, they were suggestive that the two different letters could have been written by the same man.

Additionally, there are a number of similarities, not only in the handwriting, but in the style of prose employed by Phillips and Cassidy as well. Both men exhibited a consistency in beginning sentences with "and," both tended to misspell the same words, and both used the same punctuation patterns.

Ultimately, one cannot use the extant handwriting analyses to reject the hypothesis that William T. Phillips was Butch Cassidy.

Using the aforementioned considerations, a number of Butch Cassidy aficionados have attempted to discredit and dismiss William T. Phillips as Butch Cassidy. While they have garnered a great deal of support among their ranks, they have never provided conclusive evidence that the two men were not the same.

Arguments for William T. Phillips as Butch Cassidy

As with the arguments against William T. Phillips being Butch Cassidy, the claims that he might have been the famous outlaw also invite examination. Among the prevailing arguments that the two men were the same include the testimony of friends and family and Phillips's manuscript "The Bandit Invincible."

IDENTIFICATIONS MADE BY FRIENDS AND FAMILY

Although this topic has been discussed elsewhere in this book, aspects of it are worth a brief reprisal in this section.

If William T. Phillips was an impostor, is it reasonable to assume he would have fooled longtime Cassidy friends and family members? It is not. It is distinctly possible he could have tricked a few but not the dozens who reported the visits with the outlaw. To accept that Phillips fooled all of those people is simply too much to ask.

Some have claimed Phillips assumed the Butch Cassidy identity because he intended to profit from it. Such a claim is as ludicrous as believing a Cassidy impostor could have fooled so many people who knew the outlaw. Actually, Phillips never profited from his identity as Butch Cassidy—there is no evidence he ever made a dime from the connection. Phillips never went public with his claim to be Butch Cassidy. During his lifetime, with very few exceptions, it was only his family and friends who knew of his identity.

"THE BANDIT INVINCIBLE"

This manuscript, written by William T. Phillips and apparently intended to reveal the truth about the life and times of the outlaw Butch Cassidy, offers a number of compelling considerations pertinent to making a determination of whether or not the author was Cassidy.

It is clear from a reading of "The Bandit Invincible" that the author must have been present during the occurrence of many, if not all, of the events recorded therein. The only alternative explanation would be that Phillips immersed himself in a study of Butch Cassidy, his associates, his activities, and the Wild Bunch so totally that it compared to that of any past or present Wild Bunch scholar. His research into the topic would have taken him to the archives of small newspapers and to interviews with dozens of Cassidy contemporaries. This did not happen. While Phillips was a literate man, it was clear from his writing, and from the testimony of others, that he was not well educated in the formal sense.

If Phillips was an imposter, why did he not simply use the real names of some of the people he wrote about in "The Bandit Invincible" instead of providing them with aliases? An explanation that has been offered is that, at the time, he sought to protect some of his former companions who were still alive, or relatives of the same. This is what Butch Cassidy would have done. A man who was merely assuming the identity of Cassidy, and who wanted others to believe he was Cassidy, would have used the real names of participants.

Phillips wrote about geographic locations oft frequented by the Wild Bunch. He also wrote about obscure places few people would have known about had they not lived there at the time and with those involved. In order to have described the geographic locations as he did, Phillips had to have ridden or walked many of the trails during the time certain events happened. His detailed descriptions of people, places, things, and the time period are too precise and too intimate to have been derived from contemporary resources.

Phillips also showed an intimacy and insight with the process and timing of Wild Bunch robberies that, many claim, could only have come from being a participant. Events relating to the Tipton train robbery were never described more clearly, accurately, or completely than by Phillips. It appears from reading "The Bandit Invincible" that, if William T. Phillips was not Butch Cassidy, he most certainly was present in some other capacity during the occurrence of many of the events therein related.

In "The Bandit Invincible," Phillips spoke of close friends and acquaintances Western historians never knew about. Following an investigation, however, it was discovered that Phillips was correct and the "official" historical record up to that time as it related to Butch Cassidy was incomplete.

Phillips also knew about and accurately described tiny towns in South America that had little or no significance to anyone except that Butch Cassidy visited them.

Phillips's account of what occurred relative to the Aramayo mine payroll robbery and subsequent events differs markedly with Arthur Chapman's interpretation, which had appeared approximately four to five years prior to Phillips writing his manuscript. If Phillips were an impostor, and if he wanted others to believe he was Butch Cassidy, why would he not simply have parroted much of Chapman's popularly accepted but erroneous descriptions of events, people, and places? Instead, he provided completely new and different insights into what occurred in Bolivia.

The business of William T. Phillips is a confusing one. Why is his identity prior to 1908 a mystery? Who was he? Could it be only coincidence that Phillips appeared about the time Cassidy allegedly died in Bolivia? Could it be only a coincidence that Phillips looked amazingly like Cassidy? Could it only be a coincidence that both Phillips and Cassidy possessed deep-set blue eyes and a square jaw; were outgoing, generous, and intensely loyal to friends; and had a good sense of humor? Could it only be a coincidence that the man identified by family and friends as Butch Cassidy who visited during the 1920s and 1930s gave his alias as William Phillips? Could it be only a coincidence that William Lundstrom, Phillips's closest friend and neighbor in Spokane, was also a friend of Butch Cassidy's in Wyoming during the 1890s? Could it only be a coincidence that Phillips presented a gift to Lundstrom of a pistol, on the grips of which were carved a reverse E Box E brand that was Cassidy's? Could it be only a coincidence that Phillips manifested impressive acrobatic skills on a bicycle similar to those attributed to Butch Cassidy? Could it be only a coincidence that, in addition to looking like Butch Cassidy and being identified as Butch Cassidy by family and friends, Phillips knew so much about the history, life, and times of the famous outlaw, as well as those of his close friends?

Could all of the above be coincidence? It is almost too much for one to accept, but some insist on maintaining they are nothing more than coincidence. However, experienced researchers and investigators don't believe in coincidence.

There are a number of perplexing elements associated with the hypothesis that William T. Phillips could have been the outlaw Butch Cassidy.

First and foremost, it must be remembered that all of the above is evidence, not proof beyond a reasonable doubt. There is always the possibility that this evidence, along with other, could lead to proof, but at this late date, it is doubtful this standard will ever be achieved.

Therefore, one must examine and interpret the quality of the evidence available. Frankly, given all of the previously mentioned evidence, it is difficult to dismiss a Phillips-Cassidy connection on the basis of logic and reasoning. Furthermore, when one compares the logic and abundance of the evidence associated with Phillips being Cassidy with the evidence relating to the death of Cassidy at San Vicente, the latter falls far short of substantial. The evidence for William T. Phillips being Butch Cassidy is considerably more substantial and compelling than the evidence for Cassidy having been killed in Bolivia.

There are aspects of the Phillips-Cassidy identity that are also bothersome and frustrating. One of the most disturbing is that Phillips died in 1937, yet appearances by a man identified as Butch Cassidy continued until 1941.

Could there, then, have been more than one Butch Cassidy claimant? At least one researcher believes there might have been as many as three. It is indeed a conundrum.

Following an analysis of all of the available evidence relative to the hypotheses advanced, we are subsequently in a position to invoke Occam's Razor: the hypothesis with the fewest assumptions is likely to be correct.

Given all of the hypotheses relative to the so-called death and return of Butch Cassidy, Occam's Razor supports the decision to reject Cassidy's death in South America and accept his return to the United States.

Assuming Butch Cassidy returned, was he, in fact, William T. Phillips? Given the evidence presented for and against Phillips as Cassidy, a strong case can be made for this hypothesis. Lurking around the periphery of this case, however, are niggling reminders we need more evidence, evidence we hope will be forthcoming and will answer our questions, or at least clarify and support what we already believe, regardless of our belief.

Selected Bibliography

Books

Adams, Ramon. *Six-Guns and Saddle Leather: A Bibliography of Books and Pamphlets on Western Outlaws and Gunmen.* Norman: University of Oklahoma Press, 1969.

Alexander, Thomas G. *Utah: The Right Place.* Salt Lake City, Utah: Gibbs Smith Publisher, 1995.

Baars, Donald L. *Canyonlands Country.* Salt Lake City: University of Utah Press, 1993.

Baker, Pearl. *Robbers Roost: Recollections.* Logan: Utah State University Press, 1991.

———. *The Wild Bunch at Robber's Roost.* Lincoln: University of Nebraska Press, 1965.

Betenson, Lula Parker (as told to Dora Flack). *Butch Cassidy, My Brother.* Provo, Utah: Brigham Young University Press, 1975.

Bigler, David L. *Forgotten Kingdom: The Mormon Theocracy in the American West, 1847–1896.* Spokane, Wash.: Arthur H. Clarke Company, 1998.

Breihan, Carl W. *Lawmen and Robbers.* Caldwell, Idaho: Caxton Printers, 1986.

Brown, Dee. *The American West.* New York: Charles Scribner's Sons, 1994.

Burns, R. H., A. S. Gillespie, and W. G. Richardson. *Wyoming's Pioneer Ranches.* Laramie, Wyo.: Top-of-the-World Press, 1955.

Burroughs, John Rolfe. *Where the Old West Stayed Young.* New York: Morrow, 1962.

Burton, Doris Karren. *Queen Ann Bassett: Alias Etta Place.* Vernal, Utah: Burton, 1992.

Crutchfield, James A., Bill O'Neal, and Dale L. Walker. *Legends of the Wild West.* Lincolnwood, Ill.: Publications International, 1995.

DeJournette, Dick, and DeJournette, Daun. *One Hundred Years of Brown's Park and Diamond Mountain.* Vernal, Utah: DeJournette Enterprises, 1996.

Drago, Gail. *Etta Place: Her Life and Times with Butch Cassidy and the Sundance Kid.* Plano: Republic of Texas Press, 1996.

Ernst, Donna B. *From Cowboy to Outlaw: The True Story of Will Carver.* Sonora, Tex.: Sutton County Historical Society, 1995.

———. *Sundance: My Uncle.* College Station, Tex.: Creative Publishing, 1992.

Fetter, Richard L., and Suzanne Fetter. *Telluride: From Pick to Powder.* Caldwell, Idaho: Caxton Printers, 1979.

French, William. *Further Recollections of a Western Ranchman: New Mexico, 1883–1899*. New York: Argosy-Antiquarian, 1965.

———. *Some Recollections of a Western Ranchman: New Mexico, 1883–1899*. New York: Argosy-Antiquarian, 1995.

Frye, Elnora L. *Atlas of Wyoming Outlaws at the Territorial Penitentiary*. Laramie, Wyo.: Jelm Mountain Press, 1990.

Hafen, LeRoy R., and Ann W. Hafen. *Handcarts to Zion*. Glendale, Calif.: Arthur H. Clarke Company, 1960.

Hendricks, George D. *The Bad Man of the West*. San Antonio, Tex.: Naylor, 1950.

Horan, James D. *Desperate Men*. New York: Doubleday, 1949.

———. *The Gunfighters: The Authentic Wild West*. New York: Crown, 1976.

———. *The Pinkertons: The Detective Dynasty that Made History*. New York: Crown Publishers, 1967.

———. *The Wild Bunch*. New York: Signet, 1958.

Horan, James D., and Paul Sann. *Pictorial History of the Wild West*. New York: Crown Publishers, 1954.

Jameson, W.C. *Billy the Kid: Beyond the Grave*. Lanham, Md.: Taylor Trade, 2005.

Jameson, W.C., and Frederic Bean. *The Return of the Outlaw Billy the Kid*. Plano: Republic of Texas Press, 1998.

Jessen, Kenneth. *Colorado Gunsmoke: True Stories of Outlaws and Lawmen on the Colorado Frontier*. Boulder, Colo.: Pruett Publishing, 1986.

Kelly, Charles. *The Outlaw Trail: A History of Butch Cassidy and His Wild Bunch*. Lincoln: University of Nebraska Press, 1959.

Kirby, Edward M. *The Rise and Fall of the Sundance Kid*. Iola, Wisc.: Western Publications, 1983.

———. *The Saga of Butch Cassidy and the Wild Bunch*. Palmer Lake, Colo.: Filter Press, 1977.

Knowles, Thomas W., and Joe R. Landsdale. *The West that Was*. New York: Wings Books, 1993.

Kouris, Diana Allen. *The Romantic and Notorious History of Brown's Park*. Basin, Wyo.: Wolverine Gallery, 1988.

Lamb, F. Bruce. *The Wild Bunch: A Selected Critical Annotated Bibliography of the Literature*. Worland, Wyo.: High Plains Publishing, 1993.

Larson, T. A. *History of Wyoming*. Lincoln: University of Nebraska Press, 1978.

Lavender, David. *The Telluride Story*. Ridgeway, Colo.: Wayfinder Press, 1987.

LeFors, Joe. *Wyoming Peace Officer*. Laramie, Wyo.: Powder River Publishers, 1953.

McCarty, Tom. *Tom McCarty's Own Story*. Hamilton, Mont.: Rocky Mountain House Press, 1986.

McClure, Grace. *The Bassett Women*. Athens: Ohio University Press, 1985.

Meadows, Ann. *Digging Up Butch and Sundance*. Lincoln: University of Nebraska Press, 1996.

Metz, Leon Claire. *The Shooters*. El Paso, Tex.: Mangan Books, 1976.

Moran, Frank. *The Eye that Never Sleeps: A History of the Pinkerton National Detective Agency*. Bloomington: Indiana University Press, 1982.

Moulton, Candy. *Roadside History of Wyoming*. Missoula, Mont.: Mountain Press Publishing, 1995.

Nickell, Joe. *Ambrose Bierce Is Missing and Other Historical Mysteries*. Lexington: University Press of Kentucky, 1992.

O'Neal, Bill. *Encyclopedia of Western Gunfighters*. Norman: University of Oklahoma Press, 1979.

Patterson, Richard. *Butch Cassidy: A Biography*. Lincoln: University of Nebraska Press, 1998.

———. *Historical Atlas of the Outlaw West*. Boulder, Colo.: Johnson Books, 1985.

———. *The Train Robbery Era: An Encyclopedia History*. Boulder, Colo.: Pruett Publishing, 1991.

———. *Wyoming's Outlaw Days*. Boulder, Colo.: Johnson Books, 1982.

Phillips, William T. *The Bandit Invincible: The Story of the Outlaw Butch Cassidy*. Hamilton, Mont.: Rocky Mountain House Press, 1986.

Pinkerton, William A. *Train Robberies, Train Robbers, and the Holdup Men*. New York: Arno Press, 1974.

Pointer, Larry. *In Search of Butch Cassidy*. Norman: University of Oklahoma Press, 1977.

Poll, Richard D., ed. *Utah's History*. Provo, Utah: Brigham Young University Press, 1978.

Prassel, Frank Richard. *The Great American Outlaw: A Legacy of Fact and Fiction*. Norman: University of Oklahoma Press, 1993.

Sandoval, Judith Hancock. *Historic Ranches of Wyoming*. Lincoln: University of Nebraska Press, 1986.

Selcer, Richard F. *Hell's Half Acre*. Fort Worth: Texas Christian University Press, 1991.

Siringo, Charles A. *A Cowboy Detective: A True Story of Twenty-two Years with a World-Famous Detective Agency*. Lincoln: University of Nebraska Press, 1988.

———. *Riata and Spurs: The Story of a Lifetime Spent in the Saddle as Cowboy and Detective*. Boston: Houghton Mifflin, 1927.

Swallow, Alan., ed. *The Wild Bunch*. Denver, Colo.: Sage, 1966.

Trachtman, Paul. *The Gunfighters: Showdowns and Shootouts in the Old West*. New York: Time Life Books, 1974.

Waller, Brown. *Last of the Great Western Train Robbers*. South Brunswick, N.Y.: A. S. Barnes, 1968.

Warner, Matt, and Murray E. King. *The Last of the Bandit Riders*. Caldwell, Idaho: Caxton Printers, 1940.

Wilde, Pat. *Treasured Tidbits of Time*. Vol. 1. Montpelier, Idaho: Wilde, 1977.

Articles

Boren, Kerry Ross. "Tom Vernon: Butch Cassidy Came Back." *Outlaw Trail Journal* (Summer/Fall 1993).

Buck, Daniel, and Ann Meadows. "Escape from Mercedes: What the Wild Bunch Did in South America." *Journal of the Western Outlaw-Lawman History Association* (Spring/Summer 1991).

———. "The Many Deaths of Butch Cassidy." *Pacific Northwest* (July 1987).

———. "Where Lies Butch Cassidy?" *Old West* (Fall 1991).

———. "The Wild Bunch in South America: Closing in on the Bank Robbers." *Journal of the Western Outlaw-Lawman History Association* (Fall/Winter 1991).

———. "The Wild Bunch in South America: A Maze of Entanglements." *Journal of the Western Outlaw-Lawman History Association* (Fall 1992).

———. "The Wild Bunch in South America: Merry Christmas from the Pinkertons." *Journal of the Western Outlaw-Lawman History Association* (Spring 1992).

———. "The Wild Bunch in South America: Neighbors on the Hot Seat; Revelations from the Long-Lost Argentine Police File." *Journal of the Western Outlaw-Lawman History Association* (Spring/Summer 1996).

Callan, Dan. "Butch Cassidy in Southern Nevada." *Newsletter of the Western Outlaw-Lawman History Association* (Summer 1995).

Carlson, Chip. "The Tipton Train Robbery." *Journal of the Western Outlaw-Lawman History Association* (Summer 1995).

Chapman, Arthur. "Butch Cassidy." *Elks Magazine* (April 1930).

Coleman, Max. "Cassidy in Wyoming." *Frontier Times Magazine*, March 1976.

Condit, Thelma Gatchell. "The Hole-in-the-Wall." *Annals of Wyoming* (October 1955–April 1962).

Crowell, Todd. "Did Cassidy Survive Last Shootout?" *Christian Science Monitor*, June 4, 1978.

Dullenty, Jim. "Did Regan Know Phillips and Cassidy?" *Journal of the Western Outlaw-Lawman History Association* (Spring 1992).

———. "Wagner Train Robbery." *Old West* (Spring 1983).

———. "Was William T. Phillips Really Butch Cassidy?" *Westerners Brand Book*, Chicago Corral (November/December 1982).

———. "Who Really Was William T. Phillips of Spokane: Outlaw or Imposter?" *Journal of the Western Outlaw-Lawman History Association* (Fall/Winter 1991).

Ernst, Donna B. "Blackened Gold and the Wild Bunch." *Quarterly of the National Association and Center for Outlaws and Lawman History* (January-March 1994).

———. "Sundance: The Missing Years." *Old West* (Spring 1994).

Ernst, Paul D. "The Winnemucca Bank Holdup." *Wild West* (June 1998).

Flack, Dora. "Butch Cassidy: The Living Dead." *Frontier Times Magazine* (January 1981.

Francis, A. G. "The End of an Outlaw." *World Wide Magazine* (May 1913).

Griffith, Elizabeth. "Sundance Kid: The Man in the Attic." *Journal of the Western Outlaw-Lawman Association* (Spring/Summer 1966).

Haden, Willard C. "Butch Cassidy and the Great Montpelier Bank Robbery." *Idaho Yesterdays* (Spring 1971).

Hayden, Willard C. "Butch Cassidy and the Great Montpelier Bank Robbery." *Idaho Yesterdays* (Spring 1971).

Hunter, Marvin J. "The Wild Bunch of Robbers Roost." *Frontier Times Magazine* (September 1928).

Kirby, Edward M. "Butch, Sundance, Etta Place Frolicked in 'Fun City.'" *Newsletter of the National Association and Center for Outlaw and Lawman History* (Winter 1975–1976).

Kyle, Thomas G. "Did Butch Cassidy Die in Spokane? Phillips Photo Fails." *Old West* (Fall 1991).

Lacy, Steve, and Jim Dullenty. "Revealing Letters of Outlaw Butch Cassidy." *Old West* (Winter 1984).

Longabaugh, William D. "The Sundance Kid: View from the Family." *True West* (July 1984).

Martin, R. I. "A Lively Day at Belle Fourche." *True West* (April 1962).

Meadows, Ann, and Dan Buck. "The Last Days of Butch and Sundance." *Wild West* (February 1997).

———. "Showdown at San Vicente: The Case that Butch and Sundance Died in Bolivia." *True West* (February 1993).

Patterson, Richard. "Butch Cassidy's First Bank Robbery." *Old West* (Summer 1995).

———. "Butch Cassidy's 'Peaceful Years': 1889–1894." *True West* (October 1996).

———. "Did the Sundance Kid Take Part in Telluride Robbery?" *Journal of the Western Outlaw-Lawman History Association* (Summer/Fall 1994).

———. "How They Railroaded Butch Cassidy into the Wyoming Prison for a $5 Horse." *Journal of the Western Outlaw-Lawman History Association* (Fall/Winter 1995).

———. "The Pinkertons and the Train Robbers." *True West* (August 1992).

Piernes, Justo. "Butch Cassidy in Patagonia." *Clarin* [Buenos Aires] (May 2, 1970).

Reust, Francis William, and Daniel Davidson. "Daniel Sinclair Parker: Little Known Brother of Butch Cassidy, Southern Wyoming State in December of 1889." *Frontier Magazine* (December 1995–January 1996).

Reynolds, Franklin. "Winnemucca Bank Robbery." *Frontier Times Magazine* (July 1978).

Rhodes, Gayle R. "Butch Cassidy Didn't Die in an Ambush in South America." *The West* (January 1974).

Schindler, Harold. "Butch and Sundance: Where Are They? History Muddles Ending of Tale of Butch Cassidy and the Sundance Kid." *Quarterly of the National Association and Center for Outlaw and Lawman History* (April–June 1995).

Spafford, Debbie. "Ann Bassett: 'Queen of the Cattle Rustlers,'" *Outlaw Trail Journal* (Winter/Spring 1992).

Stewart, John. "Butch and Sundance Revisited." *Quarterly of the National Association and Center for Outlaw and Lawman History* (October–December 1994).

Warner, Joyce, and Steve Lacy. "Matt Warner's Daughter Meets Butch Cassidy." *Quarterly of the National Association and Center for Outlaw and Lawman History* (Spring 1982).

Index

Adams, Ramon, 156
Alaska, 140, 150
American Bankers Association (ABA), 2, 97, 100
Amoretti, Eugenio, 37, 141
Aramayo payroll robbery, 114, 116, 171; Cassidy and Longabaugh and, 103, 105–10, 160–61; eyewitness accounts of, 111–12, 113, 159–61; questions about, 118, 119–20, 130, 161. *See also* San Vicente shootout (alleged)
Argentina, 81, 88, 91–99, 102, 103, 114, 168. *See also* South America
Austin, Thomas, 97

Bad Man of the West, The (Hendricks), 157
Baker, Pearl, 51
Baldwin, Harry, 141
Baldwin, Jim, 152
Banco de la Nación, Villa Mercedes, Chile, 99
"Bandit Invincible, The" (Phillips), 151–53, 169, 170–71
bank robberies, 2, 55, 65, 84; Montpelier, 47–49; in South America, 3, 91, 98–99, 102–3; Telluride, 24–26, 61; Winnemucca, NV, 77–80, 81. *See also* Cassidy, Butch; Longabaugh, Harry A.
Baptist church, 58
Barrientos, Rene, 121
Bass, Harry, 62
Bassett, Ann, 31, 137
Bassett, Herb, 30–31
Bassett, Josie, 31, 35, 137, 138
Bassett Ranch, 30, 31–32
Bellot, Cleto, 116–17, 122
Betenson, Bill, 144, 167
Betenson, Lula Parker, 14, 26, 42, 46, 56, 61, 65, 98; alleged return to U.S. of Butch Cassidy and, 101, 134–35, 138–41, 142, 163, 167; book about Butch by, 1–2, 138, 142–44, 167–68; Butch leaving home and, 19, 139; Butch's character and, 34, 38; Maximillian Parker and, 12, 134, 138–39
Betenson, Mark, 143
B'Hat, Mary, 39
bicycle tricks, 86, 172
Billy the Kid, 4, 82, 129, 158, 166
Billy the Kid: Beyond the Grave (Jameson), 166
Bingham, Hiram, III, 114
biomedical visualization, 128
Black Hawk War, 12
Boedeker, Henry E., 41, 141
Boedeker, W. H., 141
Bolivia, 3, 4, 81, 99–103; San Vicente, 4, 105–10, 112–13, 118. *See also* Concordia Tin Mines; San Vicente shootout (alleged); South America
Bolivian Railway, 102, 103
Bolivian Railway robbery, 107
Boren, Kerry Ross, 120–21
Bowman, Henry, 149
Boyd, Frank. *See* Longabaugh, Harry A.
Boyd, Mary, 38, 142
Boyd, Will, 142
Bracken, J. K. W., 133
Brigham Young University Press, 142
Brown, Baptiste, 29

Brown, Enrique. *See* Longabaugh, Harry A.
Brown's Park, 26–27, 29–32, 34–35, 42, 45–46, 57, 76, 137
Bryant, Elijah S., 84
Buck, Dan, 107, 117, 143, 160, 161, 167, 168, 169
Bullion, Ed, 86
Bullion, Laura, 75, 84, 86, 88
Burroughs, John Rolfe, 24, 30, 35, 40, 75, 137
Burroughs Company, 150
Butch Cassidy: A Biography (Patterson), 5, 68, 100, 112–14, 118, 136, 161, 167, 169
Butch Cassidy: My Brother (Betenson), 138, 142–43
Butch Cassidy and the Sundance Kid (movie, 1969), 3, 32, 57, 142, 155
Button, Vic, 77, 78, 80, 83

Calgary and Edmonton Railway, 61
Calvert, Ada, 38
Calvert, Kirk, 38, 39
Calvert, Mary, 70
Capehart, Tom. *See* Logan, Harvey "Kid Curry"
Carpenter, E. L., 52–53, 54
Carson, Kit, 29
Carver, Will "Colonel," 50, 83, 86, 127; death of, 84; Wild Bunch and, 62, 66, 82, 88; Winnemucca bank robbery and, 77–80, 81
Casasolo, Bonifacio, 113, 115, 116, 121
Casidy, Butch. *See* Cassidy, Butch
Cassidy, Butch: activities after alleged death, 121, 133–34, 135–46, 147; alleged burial of, 109, 118–19, 121, 123, 125–31, 162; alleged death, 1937, 142, 144, 172; alleged death, 1940s, 137, 138, 144, 172; alleged death in San Vicente, 3–4, 6, 105–10, 119–23, 125, 133–34, 144, 159, 161–62, 172, 173; alleged early death, 55–56; allegedly as William T. Phillips, 141, 146, 147–53, 163–73; alleged return to U.S., 4, 5, 6, 101, 134, 135–37, 159, 162–73; appearance, 19, 72, 76, 103, 125, 166; in Argentina, 91–99; attempts to cease being an outlaw, 71–74; bank robberies and, 3, 42, 45, 46, 55, 98–99; bank robberies by, 2, 24–27, 47–49, 77–80, 81; becoming Butch Cassidy, 32–33; Bolivian tin mines and, 99–103, 135, 147; at Brown's Park, 30–32, 34–35, 45–46, 57, 76, 137; buried loot and, 49, 55, 68–69, 76, 141, 142, 150, 164; caring for people, 2, 24, 35, 38, 40, 49, 70, 79–80, 101, 135; cattle rustling, 2, 21, 33, 38, 39; character of, 1–2, 3, 19, 31, 56, 83, 100, 101–2; early life, 7, 12–13, 14, 15–20; as George Cassidy, 30–32, 41, 141, 142; handwriting analysis, 168–69; Hole-in-the-Wall Gang and, 50–51; horsemanship, 15, 18, 19, 23, 31–32, 93; horse stealing, 2, 37, 38, 39, 40–41, 43, 65; incomplete and erroneous information about life of, 4–5, 11, 57, 91, 155–56, 157; as LeRoy Parker, 54–55; marksmanship, 18, 151; Mormon church and, 14, 20; New Mexico and, 65–66, 70; New York City and, 87–88; payroll robberies, 2, 51–55, 102, 103, 136, 160–61; photoanalysis of, 165–67; prison and, 41–43, 137; respect for life during robberies, 2, 3, 48, 67, 71, 73, 75, 99, 122; as Robert LeRoy Parker, 7, 12–22; as Roy Cassidy, 27; as Roy Parker, 22–27; saving lives, 33–34, 38; South America and, 4, 5, 32, 57, 81–82, 88, 134, 139–40; in Telluride, 21–25; in Texas, 82–84, 85–87; train robberies, 2, 66–69, 70, 74–76, 88–89, 92, 103; visits to family, after alleged death, 138–40, 150; women and, 31, 38–39, 51, 83, 86; in Wyoming, 32–34, 37–43, 66–69, 81–82; in Wyoming after alleged death, 136–37, 141–42, 147, 150. *See also* Aramayo payroll robbery; Lay, Elzy; Longabaugh, Harry A.; San Vicente shootout (alleged); Wild Bunch
Cassidy, Ed. *See* Cassidy, Butch
Cassidy, George. *See* Cassidy, Butch

Cassidy, Mike, 17–19, 21, 23–24, 27, 83
Cassidy, Roy. *See* Cassidy, Butch
Castle Gate, Utah, 51–52, 54, 72, 136
cattle rustling, 17–18, 23–24, 35, 42, 62, 66, 83; Butch Cassidy and, 2, 21, 33, 38, 39
Caverly, Bob, 37, 40
Chamberlin, Jess, 141
Chandler, Howard, 169
Chapman, Arthur, 103, 106–7, 109, 111, 117, 121, 133, 144, 157, 171
Charter, Bert, 25, 133
Charter, Boyd, 137
Chile, 97, 99, 121
Chisholm Trail, 82
Cholila Valley ranch, 92–93, 94–97
Christensen, Parley P., 73
Christiansen, Willard Erastus. *See* Warner, Matt
Circleville, Utah, 13, 15, 19, 21, 26, 135, 138–39
Coleman, E. B., 46
Colorado, 21–26, 29, 39, 59, 61, 82, 85
Concha, Justo P., 115, 116, 117
Concordia Tin Mines, 99–103, 117, 147
Cook, Fred, 138
corporations, 1, 2, 35
Crouse, Charley, 30
Cruzan, Bill, 50, 75
Currie, George "Flatnose," 55, 62, 66

Davis, Lillie. *See* Hunt, Callie May
Davis, Mathilda, 94–95
Davis, Maude, 51, 70
Deadwood, SD, 61
DeJournette, Daun, 137
DeJournette, Dick, 137
DeYoung's Photography Studio, 88
"Did Butch Cassidy Die in Spokane? Phillips Photo Fails" (article, Kyle), 165
Digging Up Butch and Sundance (Meadows), 91, 112, 115, 116, 118, 119, 126, 127, 161
Dilly, Tom, 133
Dimaio, Frank, 96–97
DNA tests, 128, 129, 130
Dodge, Fred, 81, 83–84
Drago, Gail, 31, 49, 102
Dr. Pierce's Invalids Hotel and Surgical Institute, 87
Dullenty, Jim, 143, 147, 148, 164, 167
dynamite, 67, 75, 89

Elks Magazine, 106
England, 7–8
Ernst, Donna B., 58
Evans, Robert, 95, 103

Falange de los Extranjeros, 149
Farnham, Gardner L., 150
Farr, Edward, 69, 70
First National Bank of Winnemucca, 78, 80, 83
Fitzharris, Ben, 151
Flack, Dora, 168
Folsom train robbery, 69–70, 83
Fort Worth, TX, 81, 82–84
Francis, A. G., 160–61
French, William, 66

Gardiner, John, 94, 96, 97
Garrett, Pat, 4, 158
Gass, Jim, 135
Gibbon, Daniel, 94
Gillies, Annie. *See* Parker, Ann
Gillies, Robert, 12
Gillies family, 10, 12
Glass, Clement Rolla, 99–101, 147
Goldman, William, 3, 32
Gonzalez, Gil, 106, 111–12, 119
Gottsche, William, 32, 33
Gras, Joe, 32
Great Depression, 150
Grey Bull Cattle Company, 40, 41
Grimmett, Orson, 152
Grosh, E., 84–85
Gutierrez, Walter, 115

Hainer, Al, 37, 40, 41, 141
Hallman, Oliver, 58
Hampton, Victor, 118
Hanby, Buck. *See* Minor, Bob
Hanks, O. C. "Deaf Charlie," 50, 62, 88
Hans, F. M., 68
Harris, Ellen, 151
Hazen, Josiah, 68
Heistad, Oscar, 68
Hell's Half Acre, 82–83, 84

Hendricks, George D., 157
Hillman, Dan, 54–55, 149
Hillman, Fred, 54–55, 135–36
Hole in the Wall, 49–50, 62
Hole-in-the-Wall Gang, 49, 50
Horan, James D., 82, 85–86, 157
horse racing, 23, 24, 52
horse stealing, 17, 42, 59, 60, 62; Butch Cassidy and, 2, 37, 38, 39, 40–41, 43, 65
Hunt, Callie May, 84, 86, 127
Hutcheon, Enrique B., 117–18, 121, 129
Hutcheon, James, 103, 117

Idaho, 46, 80
In Search of Butch Cassidy (Pointer), 5, 163

Jenkins, Sam, 68
Johnnie, NV, 137–38
Johnson, Merrill, 145
Johnson, William G., 141
Johnson, W. S., 78, 79
Jones, Tom, 89
Jones, W. R., 66–67
Juárez, Francisco, 92

Kelly, Charles, 5, 11, 16, 157, 163–64
Kerrigan, E. K., 75
Ketchum, "Black Jack," 77, 83, 86
Kilpatrick, Ben, 50, 62, 66, 75, 82, 84–85, 86, 88, 89
King, Murray E., 144
Kirby, Edward M., 62, 138
Kitchen, John, 145
Knight, Jesse, 41
Kraft, Bert, 137
Kyle, Thomas G., 165–67

Lacy, Steve, 144
Lamorreaux, Dora, 38–39, 141, 147
Lander, WY, 37, 39, 41, 141–42, 147, 152
Langenbach, Conrad, 57–58
La Prensa, 112, 113
Last of the Bandit Riders, The (Warner), 144
Lay, Elzy, 50, 65, 94, 133, 137; bank robberies and, 47, 48, 55; character of, 31–32; as close friend of Butch Cassidy, 31–32, 37, 45–46, 55, 57; imprisonment of, 70, 71; payroll robberies, 51–52, 53–54; at Robber's Roost, 55, 62; train robberies and, 66, 69, 70
Lay, William Ellsworth. *See* Lay, Elzy
LeFors, Joe, 69, 76
Lewis, T. W., 52–53
Livesay, Gertrude. *See* Phillips, Gertrude
Logan, Harvey "Kid Curry," 50, 55, 59, 62, 65, 86, 95; alleged death of, 85; in Fort Worth, 82, 84; killings by, 66, 74; in South America (allegedly), 98, 99, 102, 103, 121, 161; train robberies and, 66–69, 75, 76, 85, 88–89, 103. *See also* Wild Bunch
Logan, Lonnie, 55, 66
Logue, Harry, 41
Longabaugh, Elwood, 58, 94
Longabaugh, Harry A.: activities after alleged death, 121, 134, 140; alleged burial of, 109, 118–19, 121, 125–31, 162; alleged death of, 3–4, 105–10, 119–23, 125, 133–34, 144, 161–62; appearance, 50, 60–61, 103, 109, 125, 127; bank robberies and, 24, 55, 61, 77–80, 81, 98–99; Butch Cassidy and, 32, 57, 59, 60, 61, 63, 77–80, 81, 82, 85; in Canada, 61–62; character of, 61, 62, 100; early life, 57, 58–59; Etta Place and, 51, 57, 62, 86, 87–88, 91–99, 100, 128, 135, 140; horsemanship, 59, 61, 93, 99; horse stealing, 59–60, 62; marksmanship, 50, 58, 62; return to U.S., 94, 96, 100, 101, 135; robberies in South America and, 3, 98–99, 102–3; South America with Butch Cassidy and, 4, 5, 32, 57, 81–82, 87, 91–103, 139–40; train robberies and, 62, 66, 68, 75, 88, 103. *See also* Aramayo payroll robbery; San Vicente shootout (alleged); Wild Bunch
Longabaugh, Harvey, 58, 87
Longabaugh, Josiah, 57, 58
Longabaugh, Samanna, 58, 87
Longenbaugh, George, 59, 61
Longenbaugh, Mary, 59

Love, Henry, 69
Lowe, Jim. *See* Cassidy, Butch
Lundstrom, William, 172

MacKnight, Crawford, 137
Madden, Bert, 25
Madden, Bill, 62
Manning, Ione, 39
Marshall Ranch and Dairy, 16–17, 18, 19, 83
Marsters, Joseph Claude, 136
mavericking, 17–18, 32
Maxwell, Santiago. *See* Cassidy, Butch
McCarty, Tom, 23, 24, 25–27, 30, 50, 59, 61
McGinnis, William. *See* Lay, Elzy
McIntosh, A. M. "Bud," 48
Meadows, Ann, 5, 125, 167; alleged burial of Cassidy and Longabaugh and, 118–19, 123; alleged death of Cassidy and Longabaugh and, 108, 109–10, 115, 116, 117, 119, 130, 143; Aramayo payroll robbery and, 112, 119, 160–61; Cassidy, Longabaugh, Etta Place in South America and, 91–92, 93, 96, 107, 130–31; exhumation of bodies at San Vicente and, 123, 125–31
Meeks, Bub, 47, 48, 49, 50, 51, 53
Mengele, Josef, 126
Mexico, 19, 70, 134, 135, 140, 149
Michigan, 148
Milton, Dave, 46
Minor, Bob, 61
Montana, 23, 59, 60, 61, 62, 88–89, 149
Montpelier, ID, 46–49
Montpelier bank robbery, 47–49
Moonlight, Thomas, 60
Morgan, Rose, 45
Mormon church, 2, 7, 8–11, 12, 13–14, 20, 23, 46–47
Morris, Josephine Bassett. *See* Bassett, Josie
Murray, Frank, 70, 114, 120

Newbury, George, 96
Newman, Paul, 3, 142
New Mexico, 65–66, 69, 70, 83, 158, 166
New York City, 87–88
Nickell, Joe, 158–59
Nixon, George S., 78, 79, 83
Nutcher, Billy, 40, 42

Occam's Razor, 159, 173
O'Day, Tom, 50, 149
Old West magazine, 165
O'Neill, Mike, 89
outlaws, 1, 17–19, 50–51, 61, 82; Brown's Park and, 26, 29–30; in South America, 91, 95, 98–99, 103; studying history of, 4–5, 143, 156–59
Outlaw Trail: A History of Butch Cassidy and His Wild Bunch, The (Kelly), 5, 11, 157

Parker, Ann, 7, 12, 14, 19, 98, 139
Parker, Ann Hartley, 7–11
Parker, Arthur, 9–10
Parker, Bill, 145
Parker, Dan, 24, 25, 26, 59
Parker, Harry S., 33–34
Parker, Mark, 138–39
Parker, Max, 167
Parker, Maximillian, 7–10, 11, 12–14, 16, 21, 22–23, 138–39, 142, 144
Parker, Pete, 134–35
Parker, Robert, 7–12
Parker, Robert LeRoy. *See* Cassidy, Butch
Parker, Roy. *See* Cassidy, Butch
Patterson, Richard, 5, 20, 31, 68, 100, 112–14, 118, 136, 161, 167, 169
payroll robberies, 2, 51–55, 91, 102, 136. *See also* Aramayo payroll robbery
Peró, Carlos, 106, 108, 111–12, 114, 119, 120, 160
Peró, Mariano, 108, 119
Perry, Juan Commodore, 93–94, 97
Phillips, Celia Mudge, 148
Phillips, Gertrude, 148–49, 150, 163–65
Phillips, Laddie J., 148
Phillips, William Richard (Billy), 150, 164
Phillips, William T.: as Cassidy's alias on return to U.S., 146, 148, 163–73; handwriting analysis, 168–69;

photoanalysis of, 165–67; research on, 147–53. *See also* Cassidy, Butch
Phillips Manufacturing Company (PMC), 150
Phinburg, Beulah. *See* Walker, Maud
photoanalysis methods, 166
Pinkerton, Robert, 96–97
Pinkerton, William A., 85
Pinkerton National Detective Agency, 60, 86, 127; alleged death of Butch Cassidy and, 133, 134; bank robberies and, 80, 81, 84; in South America, 92, 95–98, 100–101, 102, 121, 139; train robberies and, 66, 68, 69, 70, 85; "wanted" posters and, 84, 87–88, 95, 97
Place, Annie, 57
Place, Etta, 51, 57, 86, 87, 101, 103; in Argentina, 91–99; return to U.S., 94, 96, 97, 100, 128, 135. *See also* Longabaugh, Harry A.
Place, Harry. *See* Longabaugh, Harry A.
Pleasant Valley Coal Company (PVCC), 51–53
Pointer, Larry, 5, 18, 32, 39, 100, 135–36, 137, 143; Phillips research and, 141, 147–48, 151–52, 163, 168
Porter, Fannie, 85–86
Porter, Mary, 83, 85
Powers, Orlando W., 48, 72–73
Prassel, Frank Richard, 157
Preston, Douglas A., 33, 41, 46, 48, 49, 56, 74, 134

Ralston, Wilmer, 58
Rathbone, C. E., 41
Redford, Robert, 3, 142
Rhodes, O. E., 39
Riblet Tramway Company, 150
Richards, W. A., 42, 66, 72
Rio Gallegos Banco de Londres y Tarapacá, 98–99
Rise and Fall of the Sundance Kid, The (Kirby), 62
Risso, Froilan, 115–16, 118
Robber's Roost, 50–51, 52, 55, 62
Roberts, Will, 50
Roberts, William Henry, 129, 166
Robertson, Allan, 147
Robertson, Bill, 147
Rock Springs, WY, 32, 33–34, 48, 74, 136, 137
Rogers, Annie, 86
Roosevelt, Theodore, 82
Rose, Della. *See* Bullion, Laura
Rose, George, 79
Rough Riders, 72
Ryan, James, 59–60. *See also* Cassidy, Butch
Ryan, Pat, 15–16
Ryan, Santiago. *See* Cassidy, Butch

Sadler, Lewis, 128–29
Salt Lake City Tribune, 144–45
Sanchez, Remigio, 112–13
San Miguel Valley Bank, 24, 61
San Vicente, Bolivia, 4, 105–10, 112–13, 118
San Vicente shootout (alleged), 140, 144, 148; exhumation of bodies from, 125–31; eyewitness accounts of, 113–18; legends of, 106–10, 111; questions about, 3–4, 5–6, 119–23, 133, 159, 172; versions and interpretations of, 157, 161–62
Sayles, O. W., 69
Saylor, W. O. *See* Sayles, O. W.
Schnauber, Otto, 32
Schwartz, John, 83–84
Seibert, Percy, 100–102, 103, 107, 109, 114, 143
Simpson, John, 38
Simpson, Margaret, 38
Simpson, Will, 137
Siringo, Charles A., 69
Snow, Clyde, 126–27, 128, 129, 130
South America, 171; Pinkerton National Detective Agency in, 92, 95–98, 100–101, 102, 121, 139; robberies in, 3, 98–99, 102–3; U.S. outlaws in, 91, 95, 98–99, 103. *See also* Cassidy, Butch; Longabaugh, Harry A.
Southern Pacific Railroad, 79, 84
Spence, Lowell, 85
Staunton, Dick, 46
Staunton, Ike, 46
Stough, Charles, 41, 71–72
Sundance Kid. *See* Longabaugh, Harry A.
Swift, Bob, 46
Swisher, James, 61

Taylor, John, 136
telegraph, 53, 54
Telluride, CO, 19, 21–22
Telluride bank robbery, 24–25, 61
Texas, 81, 82, 84, 85
Thornhill, Jim, 88
Tipton train robbery, 74–76, 77, 89, 102, 171
Torres, Victor, 116
train robberies, 2, 26, 62, 65, 83, 84–85, 86, 95; Folsom train robbery, 69–70, 83; Tipton train robbery, 74–76, 77, 89, 102, 171; Wagner train robbery, 88–89, 92; Wilcox train robbery, 66–69, 75, 102
Trousdale, David, 85
True West, 143
Tyler, John, 68

Union Pacific Railroad (UPR), 2, 66, 68, 69, 73–74, 75–76, 85, 97
Upson, Ashmon, 4
Utah, 8–9, 11, 26, 46, 49, 72–73, 98, 134–35, 140, 145, 150; Butch Cassidy's early life and, 7, 12–14, 15–20, 83. *See also* Castle Gate, Utah; Circleville, Utah; Robber's Roost
Utah State Penitentiary, 49

Vernon, Tom, 136

Wagner train robbery, 88–89, 92
Walker, Joe, 51, 53, 55
Walker, Maud, 86
Walker, Tacetta B., 141
Wall, Bill, 46
Wallenstine, Henry, 75
Walters, Ray, 114, 120
Ward, John, 56, 71, 72
Warner, Joyce, 144
Warner, Matt, 23–27, 48–49, 59, 61, 72, 74, 133; autobiography of, 50, 144; at Brown's Park, 30, 32, 45–46. *See also* Wild Bunch
Washington State, 4, 140, 141, 148, 149–51, 164, 168
Welch, Tom, 136
Wells, Heber M., 73
Wells Fargo and Company, 81, 83, 84
Where the Old West Stayed Young (Burroughs), 24, 40
Wilcox train robbery, 66–69, 75, 102
Wild Bunch, 5, 72, 88, 136; bank robberies by, 25, 65; cattle rustling, 38, 39; Harry Longabaugh and, 59, 60, 62; origination of, 35; Phillips's manuscript and, 149, 152, 170, 171; robbery techniques of, 3, 66, 75, 76, 79, 89, 95; in Texas, 81, 82–84, 86; train robberies, 65, 66–69, 70, 74–76, 84–85, 88–89, 95
Wild Bunch, The (Horan), 85–86
Wild Bunch at Robber's Roost, The (Baker), 51
Wilde, Pat, 48
Wilson, William, 95, 103
Winnemucca, NV, 77–80, 81, 83
Woodcock, Ernest Charles, 67, 75, 76, 102
World's Fair at St. Louis (1904), 96
Worley, John, 42
Wyoming, 23, 70, 71–72, 81–82, 84, 136–37, 149, 150, 151; Hole in the Wall, 49–50, 62; Sundance, 59–60; Tipton train robbery, 74–76, 77, 89, 102, 171; Wilcox train robbery, 66–69, 75, 102. *See also* Lander, WY; Rock Springs, WY
Wyoming State Penitentiary, 39, 41, 65
Wyoming State Tribune, 40
Wyoming Territorial Prison, 60

Young, Brigham, 8, 9, 46, 47

Zimmer, Gustav, 130
Zimmerman, Jeannine, 168

About the Author

W.C. Jameson is the award-winning author of more than seventy books, 1,500 articles and essays, one musical, three hundred songs, and dozens of poems. He has written the sound tracks for three films and appeared in five. He has appeared on the History Channel, the Discovery Channel, the Travel Channel, *Nightline*, and PBS. When not on the road conducting writing workshops and performing his music at folk festivals, roadhouses, and college campuses, Jameson is working on his next book at his home in Llano, Texas.

www.ingramcontent.com/pod-product-compliance
Lightning Source LLC
Chambersburg PA
CBHW021436100425
24897CB00006B/130

* 9 7 8 1 6 3 0 7 6 0 3 8 0 *